Cupcakes

igloobooks

Published in 2014
by Igloo Books Ltd
Cottage Farm
Sywell
NN6 0BJ
www.igloobooks.com

Food photography and recipe development: PhotoCuisine UK
Back cover images © PhotoCuisine UK

Cover image: Ruth Black/iStock/Thinkstock

FIR003 0714
2 4 6 8 10 9 7 5 3 1
ISBN 978-1-78343-465-7

Printed and manufactured in China

Contents

Classics 6

Indulgent........................ 52

Novelty 108

Special occasions 164

Classics

Raspberry Yoghurt Cupcakes

Ingredients

110 g / 4 oz / ⅔ cup self-raising flour, sifted

110 g / 4 oz / ½ cup margarine, softened

110 g / 4 oz / ½ cup caster (superfine) sugar

1 tsp vanilla extract

2 large eggs

a pinch of salt

To Decorate

12 raspberries

½ tsp pink edible glitter

175 g / 6 oz / ¾ cup unsalted butter, softened

125 g / 4 ½ oz / 1 cup icing (confectioners') sugar

4 tbsp thick vanilla yogurt

1 tsp vanilla extract

a few drops of white icing food dye

Makes

Preparation Time (Minutes)

Cooking Time (Minutes)

Method

- Preheat the oven to 180°C (160°C fan) / 350F / gas 4.

- Line a 12-hole cupcake tin with 12 cupcake cases.

- Beat together all the ingredients for the batter in a mixing bowl for 2 minutes until smooth and creamy.

- Divide evenly between the paper cases before rapping the tin on a work surface to help settle the batter.

- Bake for 15–18 minutes until risen; test with a wooden toothpick, if it comes out clean, the cakes are done.

- Remove to a wire rack to cool as you prepare the vanilla buttercream.

- Beat the softened butter for 3–4 minutes until creamy and pale.

- Add the icing sugar, vanilla yoghurt, vanilla extract and a few drops of white icing food dye before beating again until smooth.

- Spoon into a piping bag fitted with a petal tip before piping petals on top to form roses.

- Garnish with a light dusting of the glitter and a raspberry in the middle.

White Choc Chip Dream Cupcakes

Ingredients

2 eggs

250 ml / 9 fl. oz / 1 cup milk

100 g / 3 ½ oz / ½ cup granulated sugar

100 g / 3 ½ oz / ½ cup brown sugar

1 tsp vanilla extract

400 g / 14 oz / 3 cups plain (all purpose flour)

4 tsp baking powder

1 tsp salt

150 g / 5 ½ oz / 1 ¼ cup white chocolate

To Decorate

125 g / 4 ½ oz / ½ cup butter, unsalted, softened

300 g / 10 ½ oz / 2 ½ cups icing (confectioners') sugar

½ tsp vanilla extract

½ tbsp. milk

White chocolate drops

12

Makes

30

Preparation Time
(Minutes)

25

Cooking Time
(Minutes)

Method

- Preheat the oven to 200°C (180°C fan) / 400F / gas 6 and line a cupcake tin with paper cases.

- Place the eggs, vanilla extract, sugars and milk in a large mixing bowl and beat together.

- In another bowl place the flour, salt and baking powder and mix thoroughly.

- Chop the chocolate into small pieces, and stir into the flour. Pour in the liquid, and mix together until just blended.

- Spoon cupcake mix into each paper case.

- Bake, for 20–25 minutes. Test with a wooden toothpick, if it comes out clean, the cake is done.

- Place on wire rack to cool.

- To make buttercream beat butter with a whisk until soft gradually beat in icing sugar, vanilla and milk.

- Pipe buttercream swirls onto each cake. Place a chocolate drop on top.

Red-Sugar Cakes

Ingredients

125 g / 4 ½ oz / ½ cup butter
  unsalted, softened

125 g / 4 ½ oz / ½ cup light
  muscovado sugar

2 medium eggs, room temperature

125 g/ 4 ½ oz / 1 cup self-raising
  flour

2 tbsp milk

To Decorate

125 g / 4 ½ oz / ½ cup butter,
  unsalted, softened

300 g / 10 ½ oz / 2 ½ cups icing
  sugar

½ tsp vanilla extract

½ tbsp. milk

60 g / 2 oz / ¼ cup granulated sugar

red food dye

12

Makes

25

Preparation Time
(Minutes)

15

Cooking Time
(Minutes)

Method

- Preheat the oven to 200°C (180°C fan) / 400F / gas 6 and line a cupcake tin with paper cases.

- Cream butter and sugar until pale and fluffy with an electric whisk.

- Gradually mix in the eggs.

- Gently mix in the flour adding the milk.

- Spoon some cupcake mix into each paper case.

- Bake, for 15 minutes. Test with a wooden toothpick, if it comes out clean, the cakes are done.

- Place on wire rack to cool.

- To make buttercream beat butter with a whisk until soft gradually beat in icing sugar, vanilla and milk.

- Pipe buttercream onto each cake.

- Dye some sugar with a couple of drops of red food dye and sprinkle onto the buttercream topping.

Jelly Sweet Temptation Cupcakes

Ingredients

125 g / 4 ½ oz / ½ cup butter unsalted, softened

125 g / 4 ½ oz/ ½ cup caster (superfine) sugar

2 eggs

1 tsp vanilla extract

125 g/ 4 ½ oz / 1 cup self-raising flour

200 g/ 7 oz / 1 ½ cup strawberry jam (jelly)

To Decorate

125 g / 4 ½ oz / ½ cup butter, unsalted, softened

300 g / 10 ½ oz / 2 ½ cups icing (confectioners') sugar

½ tsp vanilla extract

½ tbsp. milk

jelly sweets

12

Makes

30

Preparation Time
(Minutes)

20

Cooking Time
(Minutes)

Method

- Preheat the oven to 180°C (160°C fan) / 350F / gas 4 and line a cupcake tin with paper cases.

- Cream the butter and sugar until pale and fluffy with an electric whisk.

- Gradually mix in the egg and vanilla extract.

- Gently mix in the flour adding the milk.

- Spoon some cupcake mix into each paper case.

- Bake, for 18-20 minutes. Test with a wooden toothpick, if it comes out clean, the cakes are done.

- Place on a wire rack to cool.

- With an apple corer bore out 1 ½ cm deep holes in the tops of the cupcakes.

- Fill each hole with 1 tsp of jam.

- To make the buttercream beat the butter with a whisk until soft and gradually beat in the icing sugar, vanilla and milk.

- Pipe buttercream swirls onto each cake. Place a jelly sweet on top.

Choco-Vanilla Cupcakes

Ingredients

125 g / 4 ½ oz / ½ cup butter unsalted, softened

125 g / 4 ½ oz / ½ cup caster (superfine) sugar

2 medium eggs, room temperature

½ tsp vanilla extract

125 g / 4 ½ oz / 1 cup self-raising flour

2 tbsp cocoa

45 ml / 1 ½ fl. oz / ¼ cup milk

To Decorate

125 g / 4 ½ oz / ½ cup butter, unsalted, softened

300 g / 10 ½ oz / 2 ½ cups icing (confectioners') sugar

½ tsp vanilla extract

½ tbsp. milk

chocolate balls

12

Makes

15

Preparation Time
(Minutes)

Method

- Preheat the oven to 180°C (160°C fan) / 350F / gas 4 and line a cupcake tin with paper cases.

- Cream the butter and sugar until pale and fluffy with an electric whisk.

- Gradually mix in the egg and vanilla extract.

- Gently mix in the flour and cocoa, adding the milk.

- Spoon some cupcake mix into each paper case.

- Bake, for 18–20 minutes. Test with a wooden toothpick, if it comes out clean, the cakes are done.

- Place on wire rack to cool.

- To make the buttercream beat the butter with a whisk until soft and gradually beat in the icing sugar, vanilla and milk.

- Pipe buttercream cushions onto each cake. Place a chocolate ball on top of each cake.

18–20

Cooking Time
(Minutes)

Vanilla Chocolate Cupcakes

Ingredients

150 g / 5 ½ oz / ½ cup unsalted
   butter, softened

150 g / 5 ½ oz / ½ cup caster
   (superfine) sugar

3 medium eggs

150 g / 5 ½ oz / 1 ¼ cups self-raising
   flour

60 g / 2 oz / ½ cup good quality
   white chocolate

60 g / 2 oz / ½ cup good quality dark
   chocolate

1 tbsp cocoa powder

To Decorate

125 g / 4 ½ oz / ½ cup butter

300 g / 10 ½ oz / 1 ¼ cup icing
   (confectioners') sugar

½ tsp vanilla extract

½ tbsp. milk

rose decoration

14

Makes

30

Preparation Time
(Minutes)

30

Cooking Time
(Minutes)

Method

- Preheat oven to 160°C (140°C fan) / 325F / gas 3 and line cupcake tins with paper cases.

- Cream the butter and sugar together until light and fluffy.

- Gradually mix in the eggs and flour.

- Divide the batter into two bowls.

- Melt the white chocolate in microwave. Combine with the batter in one of the bowls. Repeat with the dark chocolate and combine with the batter in the other bowl.

- Spoon a small amount of white chocolate batter into the bottom of each cupcake case. Top with a small amount of dark chocolate batter to each case.

- Repeat like this until all the batter has been used. Bake for 30 minutes. Test with a wooden toothpick, if it comes out clean, the cakes are done. Leave to cool.

- To make the buttercream beat the butter with a whisk until soft and gradually beat in the icing sugar, vanilla and milk.

- Pipe buttercream swirls onto each cake. Place a rose decoration on top of each cup.

Lemon and Poppy Seed Stars

Ingredients

150 g / 5 ½ oz / ½ cup butter, unsalted, softened

150 g / 5 ½ oz / ½ cup golden caster (superfine) sugar

3 eggs

150 g / 5 ½ oz / 1 cup self-raising flour

1 tsp lemon (grated zest)

30 g / 1 oz / ¼ cup poppy seeds

3 tbsp yoghurt

1 lemon (juice)

3 tbsp golden caster (superfine) sugar

1 tsp baking powder

To Decorate

125 g / 4 ½ oz / ½ cup butter, unsalted, softened

300 g / 10 ½ oz / 2 ½ cups icing (confectioners') sugar

½ tsp lemon extract

½ tbsp. milk

fondant stars

12

Makes

30

Preparation Time (Minutes)

20-25

Cooking Time (Minutes)

Method

- Preheat the oven to 180°C (160°C fan) / 350F / gas 4 and line a cupcake tin with paper cases.

- Cream the butter and sugar until pale and fluffy with an electric whisk.

- Gradually mix in the eggs.

- Gently mix in the flour, baking powder, lemon zest, poppy seeds and yoghurt until smooth.

- Spoon cupcake mix into each paper case.

- Bake, for 20–25 minutes. Test with a wooden toothpick, if it comes out clean, the cakes are done.

- Warm the lemon juice with the sugar in a small pan until the sugar has dissolved. With a toothpick make a few holes in the cupcake and spoon a little of the juice over each cake.

- Place on a wire rack to cool.

- To make the buttercream beat the butter with a whisk until soft and gradually beat in the icing sugar, vanilla and milk.

- Pipe buttercream and add a fondant star.

Vanilla Cream Raspberry Cupcakes

Ingredients

125 g / 4 ½ oz / ½ cup butter
unsalted, softened

125 g / 4 ½ oz / ½ cup caster
(superfine) sugar

2 medium eggs, room temperature

½ tsp vanilla extract

125 g / 4 ½ oz / 1 cup self-raising flour

2 tbsp cocoa

45 ml / 1 ½ fl. oz / ¼ cup milk

To Decorate

125 g / 4 ½ oz / ½ cup butter,
unsalted, softened

300 g / 10 ½ oz / 2 ½ cups icing
(confectioners') sugar

½ tsp vanilla extract

½ tbsp. milk

raspberries

1 drop of red food dye

12

Makes

15

Preparation Time
(Minutes)

18–20

Cooking Time
(Minutes)

Method

- Preheat the oven to 180°C (160°C fan) / 350F / gas 4 and line a cupcake tin with paper cases.

- Cream the butter and sugar until pale and fluffy with an electric whisk.

- Gradually mix in the eggs and vanilla extract.

- Gently mix in the flour and cocoa, adding the milk.

- Spoon some cupcake mix into each paper case.

- Bake, for 18–20 minutes. Test with a wooden toothpick, if it comes out clean, the cakes are done.

- Place on a wire rack to cool.

- To make the buttercream beat the butter with a whisk until soft and gradually beat in the icing sugar, vanilla, food dye and milk.

- Pipe buttercream onto each cake and top with a raspberry.

Summer Fruits Cupcakes

Ingredients

55 g / 2 oz / ¼ cup low fat spread

55 g / 2 oz / ¼ cup half spoon granulated sugar

1 egg

85 g / 3 oz / ½ cup self-raising flour

2 tbsp unsweetened apple puree

To Decorate

1 small tub crème fraiche

6 raspberries

6 blueberries

½ large banana sliced

Makes

Preparation Time (Minutes)

Cooking Time (Minutes)

Method

- Preheat the oven to 180°C (160°C fan) / 350F / gas 4 and line a cupcake tin with paper cases.

- Cream the low fat spread and sugar until pale and fluffy with an electric whisk.

- Gradually mix in the egg.

- Gently mix in the flour and apple puree.

- Spoon some cupcake mix into each paper case.

- Bake, for 12–15 minutes. Test with a wooden toothpick, if it comes out clean, the cakes are done.

- Place on a wire rack to cool.

- Spoon crème fraiche onto each cake and place the fruit on top of the cupcakes.

Blueberry Dream Cupcakes

Ingredients

150 g / 5 ½ oz / 1 ¼ cup plain (all purpose) flour
½ tsp baking powder
½ tsp bicarbonate of (baking) soda
55 g / 2 oz / ¼ cup butter softened
115 g / 4 oz / ½ cup caster (superfine) sugar
½ tsp vanilla extract
1 egg, beaten
125 ml / 4 ½ oz / ½ cup buttermilk
100 g / 4 oz / 1 cup blueberries

To Decorate

125 g / 4 ½ oz / ½ cup butter
300 g / 10 ½ oz / 2 ½ cups icing (confectioners') sugar
½ tsp vanilla extract
½ tbsp. milk
blueberries

12

Makes

15

Preparation Time
(Minutes)

15–20

Cooking Time
(Minutes)

Method

- Preheat the oven to 180°C (160°C fan) / 350F / gas 4 and line a cupcake tin with paper cases.

- Sift the flour, baking powder and bicarbonate of soda together into a bowl.

- Cream the butter and sugar together until pale and fluffy. Add the vanilla essence, egg and a spoonful of flour and mix.

- Add a third of the flour along with a third of the buttermilk and mix again. Repeat the process again twice until you have used all the flour and buttermilk.

- Spoon cupcake mix into each paper case and divide the blueberries evenly between the cakes scattering them on top.

- Bake, for 15–20 minutes. Test with a wooden toothpick, if it comes out clean, the cakes are done.

- Place on a wire rack to cool.

- To make the buttercream beat the butter with a whisk until soft and gradually beat in the icing sugar, vanilla and milk.

- Pipe buttercream swirls onto each cake and top with a blueberry.

Walnut Cream Cupcakes

Ingredients

100 g / 4 oz / ½ cup butter, unsalted, softened

100 g / 4 oz / ½ cup light muscovado sugar

100 g / 4 oz / 1 cup self-raising flour

2 large eggs

2 tsp instant coffee, mixed with 100ml / 3 fl. ox / ½ cup boiling water, then cooled

25 g / 1 oz / ½ cup walnut halves, chopped

pinch of salt

To Decorate

125 g / 4 ½ oz / ½ cup butter

300 g / 10 ½ oz / 2 ½ cups icing (confectioners') sugar

½ tsp vanilla extract

½ tbsp. milk

walnut halves

12

Makes

10

Preparation Time (Minutes)

20

Cooking Time (Minutes)

Method

- Preheat the oven to 180°C (160°C fan) / 350F / gas 4 and line a cupcake tin with paper cases.

- Beat the butter, sugar, flour and eggs with 4 tsp of the coffee and a pinch of salt until creamy. Stir in the chopped walnuts.

- Spoon some cupcake mix into each paper case.

- Bake, for 18–20 minutes. Test with a wooden toothpick, if it comes out clean, the cakes are done.

- Place on a wire rack to cool.

- To make the buttercream beat the butter with a whisk until soft and gradually beat in the icing sugar, vanilla and milk.

- Pipe buttercream swirls onto each cake and top with a walnut.

White Chocolate Raspberry Liquorice Cupcake

Ingredients

125 g / 4 ½ oz / 1 cup plain (all purpose) flour

125 g / 4 ½ oz / ½ cup caster (superfine) sugar

1 ½ tsp baking powder

40 g / 1 ½ oz / ⅕ cup butter, unsalted, softened

100 g / 3 ½ oz / ¾ cup white chocolate grated

1 egg

100 ml / 3 ½ fl oz / ½ cup whole milk

2 tbsp framboise liqueur

1 tbsp vanilla extract

To Decorate

125 g / 4 ½ oz / ½ cup butter

300 g / 10 ½ oz / 2 ½ cups icing (confectioners') sugar

½ tsp vanilla extract

½ tbsp. milk

pieces of raspberry liquorice

12

Makes

20

Preparation Time (Minutes)

20

Cooking Time (Minutes)

Method

- Preheat the oven to 170°C (150°C fan) / 325F / gas 3 and line a cupcake tin with paper cases.

- Mix the flour, sugar, chocolate, baking powder and butter until you have a sandy consistency.

- In a separate bowl mix milk, framboise liqueur, egg and vanilla.

- Drizzle into the flour while mixing until smooth.

- Spoon some cupcake mix into each paper case.

- Bake, for 18–20 minutes. Test with a wooden toothpick, if it comes out clean, the cakes are done.

- Place on a wire rack to cool.

- To make the buttercream beat the butter with a whisk until soft and gradually beat in the icing sugar, vanilla and milk.

- Pipe buttercream swirls onto each cake and top with a piece of raspberry liquorice.

Very Blueberry Cupcakes

Ingredients

375 g / 13 ½ oz / 3 cups plain
(all purpose) flour

400 g / 14 oz /2 cups granulated sugar

1 tbsp baking powder

¾ tsp salt

225 g / 8 oz /1 cup butter, unsalted,
softened

4 large eggs

240 ml / 8 ½ fl. oz / 1 cup whole milk

2 tsp pure vanilla extract

1 ½ cups fresh blueberries
plus 2 tbsp flour

To Decorate

225 g /8 oz / 1 cup cream cheese,
softened

225 g / 8 oz /1 cup butter, unsalted,
softened

900 g /2 lbs / 7 ¼ cups icing
(confectioners') sugar, sifted

2 tsp vanilla extract

purple food dye paste

blueberries

24

Makes

25

Preparation Time
(Minutes)

22

Cooking Time
(Minutes)

Method

- Preheat the oven to 170°C (150°C fan) / 325F / gas 3 and line a cupcake tin with paper cases.

- Combine the flour, sugar, baking powder, and salt. Add the butter, mixing until just coated with flour.

- In a medium bowl, whisk together the eggs, milk, and vanilla. With the mixer on medium speed, add the wet ingredients in 3 parts. Be sure to scrape down the sides of the bowl before each addition. Beat the batter until ingredients are thoroughly combined, but do not overbeat.

- In a medium bowl, gently toss the blueberries with 2 tbsp of flour, then carefully fold the blueberries into the batter.

- Spoon some cupcake mix into each paper case.

- Bake, for 18–22 minutes. Test with a wooden toothpick, if it comes out clean, the cakes are done.

- Place on a wire rack to cool.

- To make frosting, beat the cream cheese and butter and incorporate the icing sugar, vanilla extract and a little purple food dye.

- Pipe a swirl of buttercream onto each cake and top with a blueberry.

Date and Rum Cupcakes

Ingredients

110 g / 4 oz / ⅔ cup self-raising flour, sifted

110 g / 4 oz / ½ cup margarine, softened

110 g / 4 oz / ½ cup caster (superfine) sugar

1 tsp vanilla extract

55 ml / 2 fl. oz / ¼ cup dark rum

2 large eggs

a pinch of salt

To Decorate

225 g / 8 oz / 1 cup unsalted butter, softened

180 g / 6 oz / 1 ½ cups icing (confectioners') sugar

2 tbsp white rum

12 chopped dates, stones removed

12

Makes

10

Preparation Time
(Minutes)

18

Cooking Time
(Minutes)

Method

- Preheat the oven to 180°C (160°C fan) / 350F / gas 4.

- Line a 12-hole cupcake tin with 12 cupcake cases.

- Beat together all the ingredients for the batter apart from the rum in a mixing bowl for 2 minutes until smooth and creamy.

- Add the rum and beat again for a further minute.

- Divide evenly between the paper cases before rapping the tin on a work surface to help settle the batter.

- Bake for 15-18 minutes until risen; test with a wooden toothpick, if it comes out clean, the cakes are done.

- Remove to a wire rack to cool as you prepare the buttercream.

- Beat the softened butter for 3–4 minutes in a mixing bowl until pale and creamy.

- Add the icing sugar and white rum and beat again until smooth.

- Spoon into a piping bag fitted with a straight-sided nozzle.

- Pipe pillows of buttercream on top of the cupcakes before garnishing with pieces of chopped dates.

Double Chocolate Pillow Cupcakes

Ingredients

110 g / 4 oz / ⅔ cup self-raising flour, sifted

110 g / 4 oz / ½ cup margarine, softened

110 g / 4 oz / ½ cup caster (superfine) sugar

55 g / 2 oz / ⅓ cup cocoa powder

55 ml / 2 fl. oz / ¼ cup whole milk

2 large eggs

a pinch of salt

To Decorate

175 g / 6 oz / ¾ cup unsalted butter, softened

125 g / 4 ½ oz / 1 cup icing (confectioners') sugar

50 g / 2 oz / ⅓ cup cocoa powder

30 ml / 1 fl. oz / 2 tbsp whole milk

assorted milk chocolate decorations (stars, buttons, etc.).

edible glitter

12

Makes

10

Preparation Time (Minutes)

18

Cooking Time (Minutes)

Method

- Preheat the oven to 180°C (160°C fan) / 350F / gas 4.

- Line a 12-hole cupcake tin with 12 cupcake cases.

- Beat together all the ingredients for the batter apart from the milk in a mixing bowl for 2 minutes until smooth and creamy.

- Add the milk and beat again for a further minute.

- Divide evenly between the paper cases before rapping the tin on a work surface to help settle the batter.

- Bake for 15–18 minutes until risen; test with a wooden toothpick, if it comes out clean, the cakes are done.

- Remove to a wire rack to cool as you prepare the buttercream.

- Beat the softened butter with the cocoa powder, icing sugar and milk in a mixing bowl until smooth and creamy.

- Spoon into a piping bag fitted with a straight-sided nozzle and pipe in mounds on top of the cupcakes.

- Garnish the buttercream with a chocolate decoration and a sprinkle of edible glitter before serving.

Double Shot Cupcakes

Ingredients

110 g / 4 oz / ⅔ cup self-raising
  flour, sifted
110 g / 4 oz / ½ cup margarine,
  softened
110 g / 4 oz / ½ cup caster
  (superfine) sugar
1 tsp vanilla extract
2 large eggs
a pinch of salt

To Decorate

225 g / 8 oz / 1 cup unsalted butter,
  softened
180 g / 6 oz / 1 ½ cups icing
  (confectioners') sugar
1 tbsp boiling water
2 tsp strong instant espresso powder
1 tbsp sprinkles

12

Makes

10

Preparation Time
(Minutes)

20

Cooking Time
(Minutes)

Method

- Preheat the oven to 180°C (160°C fan) / 350F / gas 4.

- Line a 12-hole cupcake tin with 12 cupcake cases.

- Beat together all the ingredients in a mixing bowl for 2 minutes until smooth and creamy.

- Divide evenly between the paper cases before rapping the tin on a work surface to help settle the batter.

- Bake for 15–18 minutes until risen; test with a wooden toothpick, if it comes out clean, the cakes are done.

- Remove to a wire rack to cool as you prepare the buttercream.

- Beat the softened butter with the icing sugar in a mixing bowl until smooth.

- Mix together the espresso powder with the boiling water until smooth, then beat into the buttercream.

- Spoon into a piping bag fitted with a star-shaped nozzle.

- Carefully remove any peaks on the cupcakes with a serrated knife and pipe a swirled mound on buttercream on top.

- Garnish with a pinch of sprinkles.

Violet Cream Cupcakes

Ingredients

110 g / 4 oz / ⅔ cup self-raising flour, sifted

110 g / 4 oz / ½ cup margarine, softened

110 g / 4 oz / ½ cup caster (superfine) sugar

1 tsp vanilla extract

2 large eggs

a pinch of salt

To Decorate

225 g / 8 oz / 1 cup unsalted butter, softened

180 g / 6 oz / 1 ½ cups icing (confectioners') sugar

1 tsp vanilla extract

a few drops of purple food dye

1 tbsp purple sugar crystals

12

Makes

10

Preparation Time
(Minutes)

18

Cooking Time
(Minutes)

Method

- Preheat the oven to 180°C (160°C fan) / 350F / gas 4.

- Line a 12-hole cupcake tin with 12 cupcake cases.

- Beat together all the ingredients for the batter in a mixing bowl for 2 minutes until smooth and creamy.

- Divide evenly between the paper cases before rapping the tin on a work surface to help settle the batter.

- Bake for 15–18 minutes until risen; test with a wooden toothpick, if it comes out clean, the cakes are done.

- Remove to a wire rack to cool as you prepare the buttercream.

- Beat the softened butter in a mixing bowl for 3–4 minutes until pale.

- Add the icing sugar and vanilla extract, beating well before spooning a quarter of it into a piping bag fitted with a straight-sided nozzle.

- Add drops of the food dye to the remaining buttercream, beating well until violet.

- Spread evenly on top of the cupcakes using a small palette knife.

- Pipe a blob of icing from the piping bag on top and garnish with a sprinkle of sugar crystals.

White-Choc Coffee Cupcakes

Ingredients

110 g / 4 oz / ⅔ cup self-raising flour, sifted

110 g / 4 oz / ½ cup margarine, softened

110 g / 4 oz / ½ cup caster (superfine) sugar

1 tsp vanilla extract

2 large eggs

a pinch of salt

To Decorate

175 g / 6 oz / ¾ cup unsalted butter, softened

125 g / 4 ½ oz / 1 cup icing (confectioners') sugar

1 tsp vanilla extract

a few drops of white icing dye

110 g / 4 oz / ½ cup unsalted butter, softened

65 g / 2 ½ oz / ½ cup icing (confectioners') sugar

1 tbsp boiling water

½ tsp strong instant espresso powder

12 white chocolate buttons

12

Makes

10

Preparation Time (Minutes)

18

Cooking Time (Minutes)

Method

- Preheat the oven to 180°C (160°C fan) / 350F / gas 4.

- Line a 12-hole cupcake tin with 12 cupcake cases.

- Beat together all the ingredients for the batter in a mixing bowl for 2 minutes until smooth and creamy.

- Divide evenly between the paper cases before rapping the tin on a work surface to help settle the batter.

- Bake for 15–18 minutes until risen; test with a wooden toothpick, if it comes out clean, the cakes are done.

- Remove to a wire rack to cool as you prepare the vanilla buttercream.

- Beat the softened butter with the icing sugar and vanilla extract until smooth and set to one side.

- Beat together the butter with the icing sugar for the coffee buttercream; mix together the espresso powder with the boiling water before beating into the butter, making sure you leave it rippled.

- Spoon into a piping bag fitted with a straight-sided nozzle.

- Spread the tops of the cupcakes with the vanilla buttercream before piping a round of icing on top.

- Garnish with a white chocolate button.

Blueberry Cinnamon Cupcakes

Ingredients

110 g / 4 oz / ⅔ cup self-raising flour, sifted

110 g / 4 oz / ½ cup margarine, softened

110 g / 4 oz / ½ cup caster (superfine) sugar

1 tsp vanilla extract

1 tsp ground cinnamon

2 large eggs

a pinch of salt

To Decorate

225 g / 8 oz / 1 cup cream cheese

180 g / 6 oz / 1 ½ cups icing (confectioners') sugar

1 tbsp lemon juice

a few drops of blue food dye

200 g / 7 oz / 2 cups blueberries

12

Makes

10

Preparation Time (Minutes)

18

Cooking Time (Minutes)

Method

- Preheat the oven to 180°C (160°C fan) / 350F / gas 4.

- Line a 12-hole cupcake tin with 12 cupcake cases.

- Beat together all the ingredients for the batter in a mixing bowl for 2 minutes until smooth and creamy.

- Divide evenly between the paper cases before rapping the tin on a work surface to help settle the batter.

- Bake for 15–18 minutes until risen; test with a wooden toothpick, if it comes out clean, the cakes are done.

- Remove to a wire rack to cool as you prepare the icing.

- Beat the cream cheese with the icing sugar, lemon juice and drops of food dye until you have an even purple icing.

- Spoon into a piping bag fitted with a straight-sided nozzle before piping spiral swirls on the cupcakes.

- Garnish the perimeter with blueberries before serving.

Red Velvet Heart Flower Cupcakes

Ingredients

110 g / 4 oz / ⅔ cup self-raising
  flour, sifted
110 g / 4 oz / ½ cup caster
  (superfine) sugar
110 g / 4 oz / ½ cup butter, softened
2 large eggs
1 tsp ground cinnamon
1 tbsp red food dye

To Decorate

110 g / 4 oz / ½ cup cream cheese
55 g / 2 oz / ¼ cup butter, softened
110 g / 4 oz / 1 cup icing
  (confectioners') sugar
1 tsp vanilla extract
150 g / 5 ½ oz ready to roll fondant
  icing
red food dye
edible glitter

12

Makes

30

Preparation Time
(Minutes)

20

Cooking Time
(Minutes)

Method

- Preheat the oven to 190°C (170°C fan) / 375F / gas 5 and line a 12-hole cupcake tin with paper cases.

- Combine the flour, sugar, butter, eggs, cinnamon and food dye in a bowl and whisk together for 2 minutes or until smooth. Divide the mixture between the cases, then transfer the tin to the oven and bake for 15–20 minutes.

- Test with a wooden toothpick, if it comes out clean, the cakes are done. Transfer the cakes to a wire rack and leave to cool completely.

- Beat the cream cheese and butter together until light and fluffy then beat in the icing sugar a quarter at a time. Add the vanilla extract then whip the mixture for 2 minutes or until smooth and light.

- Spoon the icing into a piping bag, fitted with a large plain nozzle, and pipe some icing on top of each cake.

- Dye the fondant icing red and roll it out on a work surface that has been lightly dusted with icing sugar.

- Use a heart-shaped cutter to cut out 60 hearts and attach 5 hearts to the top of each cake like the petals of a flower.

- Cut out 12 small circles of icing and attach one to the centre of each cake.

- Use a small dry cake brush to apply a little edible glitter to the top of each cake.

Greek Yoghurt Cupcakes

Ingredients

110 g / 4 oz / ⅔ cup self-raising flour, sifted

110 g / 4 oz / ½ cup margarine, softened

110 g / 4 oz / ½ cup caster (superfine) sugar

30 g / 1 oz / 2 tbsp Greek yoghurt

1 tsp vanilla extract

2 medium eggs

a pinch of salt

To Decorate

110 g / 4 oz / ½ cup unsalted butter, softened

110 g / 4 oz / ½ cup Greek yoghurt

125 g / 4 ½ oz / 1 cup icing (confectioners') sugar

1 tbsp lemon juice

12 small sugarpaste flowers

1 tsp pink edible glitter

Makes 12

Preparation Time (Minutes) 10

Cooking Time (Minutes) 18

Method

- Preheat the oven to 180°C (160°C fan) / 350F / gas 4.

- Line a 12-hole cupcake tin with 12 cupcake cases.

- Beat together all the ingredients for the batter in a mixing bowl for 2 minutes until smooth and creamy.

- Divide evenly between the paper cases before rapping the tin on a work surface to help settle the batter.

- Bake for 15–18 minutes until risen; test with a wooden toothpick, if it comes out clean, the cakes are done.

- Remove to a wire rack to cool as you prepare the buttercream.

- Beat the softened butter for 3–4 minutes until creamy and pale.

- Add the icing sugar, Greek yoghurt and lemon juice and continue to beat until smooth.

- Spoon into a piping bag fitted with a star-shape nozzle before piping spiral swirls on the cupcakes.

- Garnish with a light dusting of the glitter and a sugar-paste flower.

Crimson Raspberry Cupcakes

Ingredients

110 g / 4 oz / ⅔ cup self-raising flour, sifted

110 g / 4 oz / ½ cup margarine, softened

110 g / 4 oz / ½ cup caster (superfine) sugar

1 tsp vanilla extract

2 medium eggs

a pinch of salt

a few drops of red food dye

3 tbsp framboise

To Decorate

175 g / 6 oz / ¾ cup unsalted butter, softened

125 g / 4 ½ oz / 1 cup icing (confectioners') sugar

1 tsp vanilla extract

a few drops of white icing dye

12 raspberries

Makes

Preparation Time (Minutes)

Cooking Time (Minutes)

Method

- Preheat the oven to 180°C (160°C fan) / 350F / gas 4.

- Line a 12-hole cupcake tin with 12 cupcake cases.

- Beat together all the ingredients for the batter apart from the food ing in a mixing bowl for 2 minutes until smooth and creamy.

- Add drops of food dye, beating well, until you have a pink batter.

- Divide evenly between the paper cases before rapping the tin on a work surface to help settle the batter.

- Bake for 15–18 minutes until risen; test with a wooden toothpick,

if it comes out clean, the cakes are done.

- Remove to a wire rack to cool as you prepare the buttercream.

- Beat the softened butter for 3–4 minutes until creamy and pale.

- Add the icing sugar, vanilla extract and a few drops of white icing dye and beat until smooth.

- Spoon into a piping bag fitted with a straight nozzle before piping pillows of buttercream on top.

- Garnish with a raspberry on top.

Indulgent

Raspberry Dream Cupcakes

Ingredients

125 g / 4 ½ oz / ½ cup butter,
   unsalted, softened

75 g / 2 ½ oz / ½ cup dark chocolate,
   broken into pieces

1 tsp instant coffee

1 tsp vanilla extract

150 g / 5 ½ oz / ¾ cup light
   muscovado sugar

2 eggs

1 tsp baking powder

225 g / 8 oz / 1 ¾ cup self-raising flour

150 ml / 5 ½ fl. oz / ½ cup water

400 g / 14 oz / 2 ½ cups raspberries

To Decorate

200 ml whipping cream, whipped

400 g / 14 oz / 2 ½ cups raspberries

3 tbs raspberry syrup

12

Makes

20

Preparation Time
(Minutes)

25

Cooking Time
(Minutes)

Method

- Preheat the oven to 200°C (180°C fan) / 400F / gas 6 and line a cupcake tin with paper cases.

- Melt butter in heatproof bowl over a saucepan of barely simmering water, ensure bowl does not touch surface of water.

- When half melted, add chocolate. When completely melted remove from the heat and stir to mix in any lumps, then allow to cool.

- Dissolve the coffee in the vanilla essence. Add this mixture and the brown sugar to the cooled chocolate and butter. When these are fully mixed together, add the eggs and mix in.

- Sift baking powder and flour into the mixture and beat. Stir in the

water a little at a time, making sure the liquid is entirely absorbed into the batter.

- Spoon some cupcake mix into the cases until half full. Place 3 raspberries on the surface of each which sink into batter.

- Fill almost to the top.

- Bake for about 25 minutes. Test with a wooden toothpick, if it comes out clean, the cake is done. Leave to cool.

- Whisk the cream with the raspberry syrup until firm. Pipe the cream onto the tops and place raspberries around the cupcakes.

Chocolate Cookies Cupcakes

Ingredients

110 g / 4 oz / ⅔ cup self-raising flour, sifted

110 g / 4 oz / ½ cup caster (superfine) sugar

110 g / 4 oz / ½ cup butter, softened

2 large eggs

2 tbsp unsweetened cocoa powder

To Decorate

100 g / 3 ½ oz / ½ cup butter, softened

200 g / 7 oz / 2 cups icing (confectioners') sugar

½ tsp vanilla extract

1 tbsp unsweetened cocoa powder

12 chocolate cookies

12

Makes

60

Preparation Time
(Minutes)

15–20

Cooking Time
(Minutes)

Method

- Preheat the oven to 190°C (170°C fan) / 375F / gas 5 and line a 12-hole cupcake tin with paper cases.

- Combine the flour, sugar, butter, eggs and cocoa powder in a bowl and whisk together for 2 minutes or until smooth. Divide the mixture between the cases, then transfer the tin to the oven and bake for 15–20 minutes.

- Test with a wooden toothpick, if it comes out clean, the cakes are done. Transfer the cakes to a wire rack and leave to cool completely.

- Beat the butter until smooth, then gradually whisk in the icing sugar and vanilla extract.

- Spoon half the mixture into a separate bowl and whisk in 1 tbsp of cocoa powder.

- Spoon the plain buttercream into one side of a piping bag fitted with a large star nozzle and spoon the cocoa buttercream into the other side.

- Pipe the buttercream into a big swirl on top of each cake and top each one with a chocolate cookie.

Popcorn Cupcakes

Ingredients

125 g / 4 ½ oz / ½ cup butter unsalted,
  softened

1 tsp vanilla extract

175 g / 6oz / 1 cup brown sugar,
  firmly packed

2 eggs

1 tbsp golden syrup

125 g / 4 ½ oz / 1 cup self-raising flour

½ tsp cinnamon

120 ml / 4 ½ fl. oz / ½ cup milk

100 ml / 3 ½ oz / 1 cup Dulce de Leche

To Decorate

125 g / 4 ½ oz / ½ cup butter, unsalted,
  softened

300 g / 10 ½ oz / 2 ½ cups icing
  (confectioners') sugar

½ tsp vanilla extract

½ tbsp. milk

100 g / 3 ½ oz / 4 cups popcorn

Makes

**Preparation Time
(Minutes)**

**Cooking Time
(Minutes)**

Method

- Place the brown sugar, water and salt into a saucepan and simmer over a medium heat until the mixture starts to darken and thicken.

- Take off the heat and add ½ tin of condensed milk and icing sugar and stir through. Place back on the heat and simmer for 3–5 minutes, stirring constantly.

- Mixture should be a thick runny consistency, if not add more icing sugar. Set aside to cool.

- Preheat oven to 170°C (150°C fan) / 325F / gas 3 and line a cupcake tin with paper cases.

- Beat the butter, vanilla and brown sugar with mixer until light and fluffy.

- Beat in the eggs one at a time; beat in the golden syrup. Fold in the sifted dry ingredients and milk.

- Fill the cupcake papers half way and make an indent in the mixture. Spoon a teaspoon of dulce de leche in the indent and place the rest of the mixture on top.

- Bake for 25–30 minutes. Test with a wooden toothpick, if it comes out clean, the cakes are done.

- Place on a wire rack to cool.

- To make the buttercream beat the butter with a whisk until soft and gradually beat in the icing sugar, vanilla and milk.

- Pipe the buttercream swirls and place thr popcorn on top.

Pretzel Mania Cupcakes

Ingredients

125 g / 4 ½ oz / 1 cup plain
   (all purpose) flour

210g / 7 ½ oz / 1 cup plus 2 tbsp
   granulated sugar

45 g / 1.5 oz / ⅓ cup plus 2 tbsp
   white drinking chocolate powder

½ teaspoon baking soda

¼ teaspoon salt

125 g / 4 ½ oz / ½ cup unsalted butter,
   melted and warm

2 large eggs

1 tsp pure vanilla extract

120 ml / 4 ½ fl. oz / ½ cup stout

To Decorate

125 g / 4 ½ oz / ½ cup butter,
   unsalted, softened

300 g / 10 ½ oz / 2 ½ cups icing
   (confectioners') sugar

½ tsp vanilla extract

½ tbsp. milk

pretzels

Makes

**Preparation Time
(Minutes)**

**Cooking Time
(Minutes)**

Method

- Preheat the oven to 180°C (160°C fan) / 350F / gas 4 and line a cupcake tin with paper cases.

- Add flour, white chocolate powder, sugar, baking soda, and salt in a bowl and mix thoroughly to combine.

- Add in the butter, eggs, and vanilla and beat on medium speed for one minute.

- Add ¼ cup of the beer into the mixture and beat for 20 seconds, add remaining beer. Beat for 20–30 seconds until the batter is smooth.

- Spoon cupcake mix into each paper case.

- Bake, for 18–22 minutes. Test with a wooden toothpick, if it comes out clean, the cake is done.

- Place on wire rack to cool.

- To make buttercream beat butter with a whisk until soft gradually beat in icing sugar, vanilla and milk.

- Pipe buttercream swirls. Top with pretzels.

Raspberry Mess Cupcakes

Ingredients

175 g / 6 ½ oz / ¾ cup butter, unsalted, softened

175 g / 6 ½ oz / ¾ cup caster (superfine) sugar

3 eggs

75 g / 2 ½ oz / ½ cup self raising flour

75 g / 2 ½ oz / 1 cup raspberries

3 tbsp milk

75 g / 2 ½ oz / ¼ cup dessicated coconut

25 g / 1 oz almonds, ground

To Decorate

125 g / 4 ½ oz / ½ cup butter

300 g / 10 ½ oz / 2 ½ cups icing (confectioners') sugar

½ tsp vanilla extract

½ tbsp milk

75 g / 2 ½ oz / 1 cup raspberries chopped

10–20 raspberries to top

10-12

Makes

15

Preparation Time (Minutes)

15–20

Cooking Time (Minutes)

Method

- Preheat the oven to 190°C (170°C fan) / 375F / gas 5 and line a cupcake tin with paper cases.

- Cream the butter and sugar until pale and fluffy with an electric whisk.

- Gradually mix in the eggs.

- Gently mix in the flour, ¾ of the raspberries and milk.

- Fold in the coconut and almonds.

- Spoon some cupcake mix into each paper case. Scatter the rest of the raspberries over the top.

- Bake, for 15–20 minutes. Test with a wooden toothpick, if it comes out clean, the cakes are done.

- Place on a wire rack to cool.

- To make the buttercream, beat butter with a whisk until soft and gradually beat in the icing sugar, vanilla, chopped raspberries and milk.

- Spoon buttercream onto the cakes and top with a whole raspberry.

Sweet Dreams Cupcakes

Ingredients

120 g / 4 ½ oz / 1 cup plain (all purpose) flour

140 g / 5 oz / ½ cup caster (superfine) sugar

1½ tsp baking powder

a pinch of salt

45 g / 1 ½ oz / ¼ cup unsalted butter, at room temperature

120 ml / 4 ½ fl. oz / ½ cup whole milk

1 egg

¼ tsp vanilla extract

12 medium pink marshmallows

To Decorate

125 g / 4 ½ oz / ½ cup butter, unsalted, softened

300 g / 10 ½ oz / 2 ½ cups icing (confectioners') sugar

½ tsp vanilla extract

½ tbsp. milk

1 packet of mini marshmallows

12

Makes

40

Preparation Time (Minutes)

20–25

Cooking Time (Minutes)

Method

- Preheat the oven to 170°C (150°C fan) / 325F / gas 3 and line a cupcake tin with paper cases

- Mix flour, sugar, baking powder, salt and butter until you get a sandy consistency.

- Gradually pour in half the milk and beat until the milk is just incorporated.

- Whisk the egg, vanilla extract and remaining milk together in a separate bowl for a few seconds, pour into the flour mixture and mix until smooth. Do not over-mix.

- Spoon some cupcake mix into each paper case.

- Bake, for 20–25 minutes. Test with a wooden toothpick, if it comes out clean, the cakes are done.

- Place on a wire rack to cool.

- Put the medium marshmallows in a heatproof bowl over a pan of simmering water. Leave until melted and smooth.

- When the cupcakes are cold, hollow out a small section in the centre of each one and fill with a dollop of melted marshmallow. Leave to cool.

- To make the buttercream beat butter with a whisk until soft and gradually beat in the icing sugar, vanilla and milk.

- Pipe buttercream onto the cupcakes. Top each cake with mini marshmallows.

Chocolate Decadence Cupcakes

Ingredients

110 g / 4 oz / ⅔ cup self-raising
  flour, sifted
110 g / 4 oz / ½ cup caster
  (superfine) sugar
110 g / 4 oz / ½ cup butter, softened
2 large eggs
2 tbsp unsweetened cocoa powder

To Decorate

100 g / 3 ½ oz / ½ cup butter, softened
200 g / 7 oz / 2 cups icing
  (confectioners') sugar
1 tbsp unsweetened cocoa powder
100 g / 3 ½ oz dark chocolate, melted
48 chocolate balls
48 chocolate buttons

12

Makes

70

Preparation Time
(Minutes)

15–20

Cooking Time
(Minutes)

Method

- Preheat the oven to 190°C (170°C fan) / 375F / gas 5 and line a 12-hole cupcake tin with paper cases.

- Combine the flour, sugar, butter, eggs and cocoa powder in a bowl and whisk together for 2 minutes or until smooth. Divide the mixture between the cases, then transfer the tin to the oven and bake for 15–20 minutes.

- Test with a wooden toothpick, if it comes out clean, the cakes are done. Transfer the cakes to a wire rack and leave to cool completely.

- Beat the butter until smooth, then gradually whisk in the icing sugar and cocoa powder.

- Spoon a quarter of the buttercream into a separate bowl and set aside.

- Fold the melted chocolate into the rest of the buttercream until smoothly combined.

- Spoon the dark chocolate buttercream into a piping bag, fitted with a large plain nozzle and pipe a swirl of buttercream on top of each cake.

- Spoon the reserved paler buttercream into a piping bag fitted with a large star nozzle and pipe a rosette on top of each dark chocolate swirl.

- Arrange 4 chocolate balls on top of each cake.

- Slide a chocolate button between each chocolate ball.

Day Dream Cupcakes

Ingredients

150 g / 5 ½ oz / 1 ¼ cup plain (all purpose) flour

300 g / 11 oz / 1 ½ cups granulated sugar

12 egg whites from large eggs

¼ tsp salt

1 ½ tsp vanilla extract

1 ½ tsp cream of tartare

To Decorate

125 g / 4 ½ oz / ½ cup butter, unsalted, softened

300 g / 10 ½ oz / 2 ½ cups icing (confectioners') sugar

½ tsp vanilla extract

½ tbsp milk

assorted little sweets

12

Makes

30

Preparation Time (Minutes)

25

Cooking Time (Minutes)

Method

- Preheat the oven to 180°C (160°C fan) / 350F / gas 4 and line a cupcake tin with paper cases.

- Place egg whites in a large mixing bowl and beat at high speed until egg whites are frothy (1 minute).

- Add the cream of tartar, salt and vanilla to the egg whites. Mix at high speed until the egg whites are almost stiff (4 minutes).

- Add 1 cup of sugar gradually while mixing on low speed.

- Mix flour and remaining sugar together and spoon ¼ of mixture over egg whites, folding gently between each addition.

- Spoon some cupcake mix into each paper case.

- Bake, for 20–25 minutes. Test with a wooden toothpick, if it comes out clean, the cakes are done.

- Place on a wire rack to cool.

- To make the buttercream beat the butter with a whisk until soft and gradually beat in the icing sugar, vanilla and milk.

- Pipe buttercream swirls onto each cake and top with assorted little sweets.

Vanilla Rose Cupcakes

Ingredients

225 g / 8 oz / 1 cup unsalted butter, softened

175 g / 6 oz / ¾ cup light muscovado sugar

3 eggs

225 g / 8 oz / 1 ½ cups self-raising flour

2 tsp ground ginger

175 ml / 6 fl.oz / ¾ cup milk

for the rhubarb compote

124 g / 4 ½ oz / 1 ¼ cup rhubarb, trimmed and cut into small dice

30 g / 1 oz / ⅛ cup golden caster (superfine) sugar

1 tsp ground ginger

1 tbsp water

To Decorate

125 g / 4 ½ oz / ½ cup butter, unsalted, softened

300 g / 10 ½ oz / 2 ½ cups icing sugar

½ tsp vanilla extract

½ tbsp. milk

12

Makes

20

Preparation Time (Minutes)

18–20

Cooking Time (Minutes)

Method

- Preheat the oven to 200°C (180°C fan) / 400F / gas 6 and line a cupcake tin with paper cases.

- Cream the butter and sugar until pale and fluffy with an electric whisk.

- Gradually mix in the egg.

- Gently mix in the flour and ginger, adding the milk.

- Spoon some cupcake mix into each paper case.

- Bake, for 18–20 minutes. Test with a wooden toothpick, if it comes out clean, the cakes are done.

- Place on a wire rack to cool.

- To make the rhubarb compote: place all the ingredients in a small pan and heat gently to boiling point (you just want the rhubarb to release its natural juices and turn a beautiful shade of pink). Leave to bubble and reduce for 2–3 minutes.

- Once the rhubarb has softened and the liquid has gone syrupy, remove from the heat and leave to cool completely.

- With an apple corer bore out 1½ cm deep hole in the tops of cupcakes. Fill with a spoonful of the compote.

- To make the buttercream beat the butter with a whisk until soft and gradually beat in the icing sugar, vanilla and milk.

- Pipe buttercream onto each cake with rose nozzle.

Chocolate Cigarillo Cupcakes

Ingredients

3 eggs

150 g / 5 ½ oz / ¾ cup granulated
sugar

200 g / 7 oz / 1 ¼ cup beetroot,
peeled and grated

½ tsp vanilla extract

180 g / 6 ½ oz /1 ½ cup plain (all
purpose) flour

180 g / 6 ½ oz / 2 cups almonds,
ground

2 tsp baking powder

2 tbsp cocoa powder

¼ tsp salt

284 ml / 10 fl. oz / 1 ¼ cup buttermilk

To Decorate

125 g / 4 ½ oz / ½ cup butter,
unsalted, softened

300 g / 10 ½ oz / 2 ½ cups icing
(confectioners') sugar

½ tsp vanilla extract

½ tbsp. milk

cigarillos

24

Makes

20

**Preparation Time
(Minutes)**

20

**Cooking Time
(Minutes)**

Method

- Preheat oven to 180°C (160°C fan) / 350F / gas 4 and line cupcake tins with paper cases.

- In a large mixing bowl, whisk up the eggs and sugar for 4 minutes until they are light and fluffy.

- Beat in the grated beetroot and vanilla essence. Add the flour, ground almonds, baking powder, cocoa powder, salt and beat until combined.

- Add the buttermilk. Beat again to ensure everything is well combined.

- Spoon some cupcake mix into each paper case.

- Bake for 20 minutes. Test with a wooden toothpick, if it comes out clean, the cakes are done. Leave to cool.

- To make the buttercream beat butter with a whisk until soft and gradually beat in the icing sugar, vanilla and milk.

- Pipe buttercream onto each cake. Place a cigarillo on top to decorate.

Chocolate Chip Cream Cupcakes

Ingredients

150 g / 5 ½ oz / ½ cup butter, unsalted, softened

150 g / 5 ½ oz / ¾ cup light muscovado sugar

3 eggs

115 g / 4 oz / 1 cup self-raising flour

35 g / 1 ½ oz / ¼ cup cocoa powder

½ tsp baking powder

100 g / 3 ½ oz / ¾ cup milk chocolate chips

To Decorate

125 g / 4 ½ oz / ½ cup butter, unsalted, softened

300 g / 10 ½ oz / 2 ½ cups icing (confectioners') sugar

½ tsp vanilla extract

½ tbsp milk

10

Makes

40

Preparation Time (Minutes)

20

Cooking Time (Minutes)

Method

- Preheat the oven to 170°C (150°C fan) / 325F / gas 3 and line a cupcake tin with paper cases.

- Cream the butter and sugar until pale and fluffy with an electric whisk.

- Gradually mix in the eggs.

- Gently mix in the flour, cocoa, vanilla, baking powder and chocolate chips.

- Spoon some cupcake mix into each paper case.

- Bake, for 20 minutes. Test with a wooden toothpick, if it comes out clean, the cakes are done.

- Place on a wire rack to cool.

- To make the buttercream beat butter with a whisk until soft and gradually beat in the icing sugar, vanilla and milk.

- Pipe buttercream onto each cake with rose nozzle.

Lemon Drop Cupcakes

Ingredients

100 g / 4 oz / ½ cup butter, unsalted, softened

100 g / 4 oz / ½ cup caster (superfine) sugar

1 tsp vanilla extract

2 eggs

100 g / 4 oz / 1 cup self-raising flour

1 lemon, unwaxed, zest only

50 g / 2 oz / ¼ cup lemon curd

To Decorate

125 g / 4 ½ oz / ½ cup butter, unsalted, softened

300 g / 10 ½ oz / 2 ½ cups icing (confectioners') sugar

½ tsp lemon extract

½ tbsp. milk

100 g / 4 oz / ½ cup granulated sugar

yellow food dye

12

Makes

15

Preparation Time
(Minutes)

15–20

Cooking Time
(Minutes)

Method

- Preheat the oven to 180°C (160°C fan) / 350F / gas 4 and line a cupcake tin with paper cases.

- Cream the butter and sugar until pale and fluffy with an electric whisk.

- Gradually mix in the eggs and vanilla.

- Gently mix in the flour and lemon zest until smooth.

- Spoon some cupcake mix into each paper case. Add 1 tsp of lemon curd to the top of each cupcake.

- Bake, for 15–20 minutes. Test with a wooden toothpick, if it comes out clean, the cakes are done.

- Warm the lemon juice with the sugar in a small pan until the sugar has dissolved. With a toothpick make a few holes in the cupcakes and spoon a little over each cake.

- Place on a wire rack to cool.

- To make the buttercream beat butter with a whisk until soft and gradually beat in the icing sugar, vanilla and milk.

- Pipe buttercream peaks onto each cupcake.

- Add a few drops of food dye to the sugar and sprinkle onto the cupcakes.

Strawberry Jam Frosted Cupcakes

Ingredients

15 g / ½ oz / ¼ cup freeze dried strawberries

150 g / 5 ½ oz / ½ cup butter, unsalted, softened

150 g / 5 ½ oz / ½ cup caster (superfine) sugar

3 eggs

150 g / 5 ½ oz / 1 cup self-raising flour

½ tsp baking powder

To Decorate

125 g / 4 ½ oz / ½ cup butter

300 g / 10 ½ oz / 2 ½ cups icing (confectioners') sugar

½ tsp vanilla extract

½ tbsp. milk

strawberry jam (jelly)

12

Makes

20

Preparation Time (Minutes)

20–25

Cooking Time (Minutes)

Method

- Preheat the oven to 180°C (160°C fan) / 350F / gas 4 and line a cupcake tin with paper cases.

- Crush the strawberries in a pestle and mortar until finely ground but not completely powdered.

- Cream the butter and sugar until pale and fluffy with an electric whisk.

- Gradually mix in the eggs.

- Add strawberries, flour and baking powder.

- Spoon some cupcake mix into each paper case.

- Bake, for 20–25 minutes. Test with a wooden toothpick, if it comes out clean, the cakes are done.

- Place on a wire rack to cool.

- To make the buttercream beat butter with a whisk until soft and gradually beat in the icing sugar, vanilla and milk.

- Pipe buttercream swirls onto each cupcake and top with 1 tsp of strawberry jam.

Banoffee Pie Cupcakes

Ingredients

125 g / 4 ½ oz / ½ cup butter
  unsalted, softened

175 g / 6 ½ oz / 1 ½ cup plain (all
  purpose) flour

30 g / 1 oz / ⅕ cup ground almonds

1 tsp baking powder

160 g/ 6 oz / ¾ cup golden caster
  (superfine) sugar

1 tsp vanilla extract

120 ml / 4 ½ fl. oz / ½ cup milk

50 ml / 2 fl. oz / ¼ cup amaretto

400 ml / 14 ½ fl. oz / 1 ¾ cup double
  cream

To Decorate

2 banana's

100 g / 3 ½ oz / ½ cup golden caster
  (superfine) sugar

100 ml / 3 ½ fl. oz / ½ cup amaretto

100 ml / 3 ½ fl. oz / ½ cup double
  (heavy) cream

1 tbsp fresh orange juice

1 vanilla pod

12

Makes

20

Preparation Time
(Minutes)

18–20

Cooking Time
(Minutes)

Method

- Preheat oven to 180°C (160°C fan) / 350F / gas 4 and line a cupcake tin with paper cases.

- Cream the butter and sugar until pale and fluffy with an electric whisk. Gradually beat in the eggs and extracts.

- Mix together the flour, ground almonds, baking powder and gradually mix in the milk. Divide the mixture between cases.

- Bake, for 18–20 minutes. Test with a wooden toothpick, if it comes out clean, the cakes are done.

- Place the tin on a wire rack. Poke holes in top of each cupcake and pour over 1 tsp of amaretto per cake. Allow to cool completely before removing from the tins.

- To decorate, heat the sugar, stirring, until it melts and turns golden brown. Add the banana and toss.

- Pour in the amaretto; immediately tilt the pan to ignite the alcohol. Allow the flames to subside and the caramel is melted. Strain away any excess liquid. Carefully stir in the orange juice, and vanilla-pod seeds. Reduce the heat to medium; bring to the boil, stirring occasionally, until thickened (about 5 minutes). Let cool completely.

- Whip the cream and spread onto the cupcakes.

- Spoon flambéed banana over the top.

Dark Chocolate Delight Cupcakes

Ingredients

125 g / 4 ½ oz / ½ cup butter
   unsalted, softened

125 g / 4 ½ oz / ½ cup caster
   (superfine) sugar

2 medium eggs, room temperature

½ tsp vanilla extract

125 g / 4 ½ oz / 1 cup self-raising
   flour

2 tbsp cocoa

45 ml / 1 ½ fl. oz / ¼ cup milk

To Decorate

125 g / 4 ½ oz / ½ cup butter,
   unsalted, softened

300 g / 10 ½ oz / 2 ½ cups icing
   (confectioners') sugar

½ tsp vanilla extract

½ tbsp. milk

50 g / 2 oz / ¼ cup very "dark"
   chocolate grated

12

Makes

20

Preparation Time
(Minutes)

18–20

Cooking Time
(Minutes)

Method

- Preheat the oven to 180°C (160°C fan) / 350F / gas 4 and line a cupcake tin with paper cases.

- Cream the butter and sugar until pale and fluffy with an electric whisk.

- Gradually mix in the eggs and vanilla extract.

- Gently mix in the flour and cocoa, adding the milk.

- Spoon some cupcake mix into each paper case.

- Bake, for 18–20 minutes. Test with a wooden toothpick, if it comes out clean, the cakes are done.

- Place on a wire rack to cool.

- To make the buttercream, beat the butter with a whisk until soft and gradually beat in the icing sugar, vanilla and milk.

- Pipe buttercream onto each cake and sprinkle with grated chocolate.

Sugared Blueberry Pie Cupcakes

Ingredients

110 g / 4 oz / ⅔ cup self-raising flour, sifted

110 g / 4 oz / ½ cup margarine, softened

110 g / 4 oz / ½ cup caster (superfine) sugar

1 tsp vanilla extract

2 large eggs

a pinch of salt

To Decorate

175 g / 6 oz / ¾ cup unsalted butter, softened

125 g / 4 ½ oz / 1 cup icing (confectioners') sugar

a few drops of purple food dye

150 g / 5 oz / 1 ½ cups blueberries

1 tbsp caster (superfine) sugar

12

Makes

10

Preparation Time
(Minutes)

15–18

Cooking Time
(Minutes)

Method

- Preheat the oven to 180°C (160°C fan) / 350F / gas 4.

- Line a 12-hole cupcake tin with 12 cupcake cases.

- Beat together all the ingredients for the batter in a mixing bowl for 2 minutes until smooth and creamy.

- Divide evenly between the paper cases before rapping the tin on a work surface to help settle the batter.

- Bake for 15–18 minutes until risen; test with a wooden toothpick, if it comes out clean, the cakes are done.

- Remove to a wire rack to cool as you prepare the vanilla buttercream.

- Beat the softened butter for 3–4 minutes until creamy and pale.

- Add the icing sugar and a few drops of food dye, beating well until light purple in dye.

- Level the top of the cupcakes before spreading evenly with the buttercream.

- Sprinkle the tops with sugar before garnishing with 6 blueberries.

Chocolate Raspberry Buttercream Cupcakes

Ingredients

110 g / 4 oz / ⅔ cup self-raising flour, sifted

110 g / 4 oz / ½ cup margarine, softened

110 g / 4 oz / ½ cup caster (superfine) sugar

55 g / 2 oz / ⅓ cup cocoa powder

55 ml / 2 fl. oz / ¼ cup whole milk

2 large eggs

a pinch of salt

To Decorate

175 g / 6 oz / ¾ cup unsalted butter, softened

125 g / 4 ½ oz / 1 cup icing (confectioners') sugar

50 g / 2 oz / ⅓ cup cocoa powder

30 ml / 1 fl. oz / 2 tbsp whole milk

12 raspberries

12

Makes

10

Preparation Time
(Minutes)

15–18

Cooking Time
(Minutes)

Method

- Preheat the oven to 180°C (160°C fan) / 350F / gas 4.

- Line a 12-hole cupcake tin with 12 cupcake cases.

- Beat together all the ingredients for the batter apart from the milk in a mixing bowl for 2 minutes until smooth and creamy.

- Add the milk and beat again for a further minute.

- Divide evenly between the paper cases before rapping the tin on a work surface to help settle the batter.

- Bake for 15–18 minutes until risen; test with a wooden toothpick, if it comes out clean, the cakes are done.

- Remove to a wire rack to cool as you prepare the buttercream.

- Beat the softened butter with the cocoa powder, icing sugar and milk in a mixing bowl until smooth and creamy.

- Spoon into a piping bag fitted with a straight-sided nozzle and pipe in swirled mounds on top of the cupcakes.

- Garnish the top of the buttercream with a raspberry before serving.

Pink Crown Raspberry Cupcakes

Ingredients

110 g / 4 oz / ⅔ cup self-raising
  flour, sifted

110 g / 4 oz / ½ cup margarine,
  softened

110 g / 4 oz / ½ cup caster
  (superfine) sugar

1 tsp vanilla extract

2 large eggs

a pinch of salt

To Decorate

150 g / 5 oz / ⅔ cup unsalted butter,
  softened

90 g / 3 ½ oz / ¾ cup icing
  (confectioners') sugar

2 tbsp Framboise

200 g / 7 oz / 2 cups raspberries

12

Makes

10

**Preparation Time
(Minutes)**

15–18

**Cooking Time
(Minutes)**

Method

- Preheat the oven to 180°C (160°C fan) / 350F / gas 4.

- Line a 12-hole cupcake tin with 12 cupcake cases.

- Beat together all the ingredients for the batter in a mixing bowl for 2 minutes until smooth and creamy.

- Divide evenly between the paper cases before rapping the tin on a work surface to help settle the batter.

- Bake for 15–18 minutes until risen; test with a wooden toothpick, if it comes out clean, the cakes are done.

- Remove to a wire rack to cool as you prepare the buttercream.

- Beat the softened butter in a mixing bowl for 3–4 minutes until pale.

- Add the icing sugar and the Framboise and beat again until smooth.

- Spoon into a piping bag fitted with a star-shaped nozzle and pipe a blob on top of each cupcake.

- Garnish the perimeter with raspberries before serving.

Chocolate Tear Cupcakes

Ingredients

110 g / 4 oz / ⅔ cup self-raising flour, sifted

110 g / 4 oz / ½ cup margarine, softened

110 g / 4 oz / ½ cup caster (superfine) sugar

55 g / 2 oz / ⅓ cup cocoa powder

55 ml / 2 fl. oz / ¼ cup whole milk

2 large eggs

a pinch of salt

To Decorate

175 g / 6 oz / ¾ cup unsalted butter, softened

125 g / 4 ½ oz / 1 cup icing (confectioners') sugar

50 g / 2 oz / ⅓ cup cocoa powder

2 tbsp whole milk

edible glitter

12

Makes

10

Preparation Time (Minutes)

15–18

Cooking Time (Minutes)

Method

- Preheat the oven to 180°C (160°C fan) / 350F / gas 4.

- Line a 12-hole cupcake tin with 12 cupcake cases.

- Beat together all the ingredients for the batter apart from the milk in a mixing bowl for 2 minutes until smooth and creamy.

- Add the milk and beat again for a further minute.

- Divide evenly between the paper cases before rapping the tin on a work surface to help settle the batter.

- Bake for 15–18 minutes until risen; test with a wooden toothpick, if it comes out clean, the cakes are done.

- Remove to a wire rack to cool as you prepare the buttercream.

- Beat the softened butter with the cocoa powder, icing sugar and milk in a mixing bowl until smooth and creamy.

- Spoon into a piping bag fitted with a straight-sided nozzle and pipe 7 small tears on top of the cupcakes.

- Garnish the buttercream with a pinch of edible glitter before serving.

Chocolate Cookies and Cream Cupcakes

Ingredients

110 g / 4 oz / ⅔ cup self-raising flour, sifted

110 g / 4 oz / ½ cup margarine, softened

110 g / 4 oz / ½ cup caster (superfine) sugar

55 g / 2 oz / ⅓ cup cocoa powder

2 tbsp whole milk

2 large eggs

a pinch of salt

To Decorate

225 g / 8 oz / 1 cup unsalted butter, softened

180 g / 6 oz / 1 ½ cups icing (confectioners') sugar

1 bourbon biscuit, crushed

6 bourbon biscuits, lightly crushed

12

Makes

10

Preparation Time
(Minutes)

15–18

Cooking Time
(Minutes)

Method

- Preheat the oven to 180°C (160°C fan) / 350F / gas 4.

- Line a 12-hole cupcake tin with 12 cupcake cases.

- Beat together all the ingredients for the batter apart from the milk in a mixing bowl for 2 minutes until smooth and creamy.

- Add the milk and beat again for a further minute.

- Divide evenly between the paper cases before rapping the tin on a work surface to help settle the batter.

- Bake for 15–18 minutes until risen; test with a wooden toothpick, if it comes out clean, the cakes are done.

- Remove to a wire rack to cool as you prepare the buttercream.

- Beat the softened butter for 3–4 minutes in a mixing bowl until pale and creamy.

- Add the icing sugar and beat again until smooth before folding through the crushed bourbon biscuit.

- Spread the tops of the cupcakes with the icing before garnishing the top with lightly crushed bourbon biscuits.

Cappuccino Cupcakes

Ingredients

110 g / 4 oz / ⅔ cup self-raising flour, sifted

110 g / 4 oz / ½ cup margarine, softened

110 g / 4 oz / ½ cup caster (superfine) sugar

55 g / 2 oz / ⅓ cup cocoa powder

55 ml / 2 fl. oz / ¼ cup whole milk

2 large eggs

a pinch of salt

To Decorate

175 g / 6 oz / ¾ cup unsalted butter, softened

125 g / 4 ½ oz / 1 cup icing (confectioners') sugar

50 g / 2 oz / ⅓ cup cocoa powder

2 tbsp whole milk

1 tbsp boiling water

1 tsp strong instant espresso powder

12 white and dark chocolate cigarillos

12

Makes

10

Preparation Time
(Minutes)

15–18

Cooking Time
(Minutes)

Method

- Preheat the oven to 180°C (160°C fan) / 350F / gas 4.

- Line a 12-hole cupcake tin with 12 cupcake cases.

- Beat together all the ingredients for the batter apart from the milk in a mixing bowl for 2 minutes until smooth and creamy.

- Add the milk and beat again for a further minute.

- Divide evenly between the paper cases before rapping the tin on a work surface to help settle the batter.

- Bake for 15–18 minutes until risen; test with a wooden toothpick, if it comes out clean, the cakes are done.

- Remove to a wire rack to cool as you prepare the buttercream.

- Beat the softened butter with the cocoa powder, icing sugar and milk in a mixing bowl until smooth and creamy.

- Mix together the espresso powder with the boiling water until smooth, then beat into the buttercream.

- Spoon into a piping bag fitted with a petal tip and pipe in folds on top of the cupcakes.

- Garnish the buttercream with a cigarillo before serving.

Lavender Pillow Cupcakes

Ingredients

110 g / 4 oz / ⅔ cup self-raising flour, sifted

110 g / 4 oz / ½ cup margarine, softened

110 g / 4 oz / ½ cup caster (superfine) sugar

1 tsp lemon extract

2 large eggs

a pinch of salt

To Decorate

225 g / 8 oz / 1 cup unsalted butter, softened

180 g / 6 oz / 1 ½ cups icing (confectioners') sugar

½ tsp vanilla extract

½ tsp edible lavender extract

a few drops of purple food dye

1 tbsp lavender sugar

12

Makes

10

Preparation Time
(Minutes)

15–18

Cooking Time
(Minutes)

Method

- Preheat the oven to 180°C (160°C fan) / 350F / gas 4.

- Line a 12-hole cupcake tin with 12 cupcake cases.

- Beat together all the ingredients for the batter in a mixing bowl for 2 minutes until smooth and creamy.

- Divide evenly between the paper cases before rapping the tin on a work surface to help settle the batter.

- Bake for 15–18 minutes until risen; test with a wooden toothpick, if it comes out clean, the cakes are done.

- Remove to a wire rack to cool as you prepare the buttercream.

- Beat the softened butter for 2–3 minutes until creamy and pale.

- Add the icing sugar and vanilla extract and beat again until smooth.

- Spoon ⅔ into a piping bag fitted with a straight-sided nozzle before adding a few drops of food dye and the lavender extract to the remaining buttercream.

- Beat well until the buttercream is violet before spreading evenly on top of the cupcakes.

- Pipe pillows of the plain vanilla buttercream on top of the cupcakes before garnishing with the lavender sugar.

Mochaccino Cupcakes

Ingredients

110 g / 4 oz / ⅔ cup self-raising
  flour, sifted

110 g / 4 oz / ½ cup margarine,
  softened

110 g / 4 oz / ½ cup caster
  (superfine) sugar

55 g / 2 oz / ⅓ cup cocoa powder

55 ml / 2 fl. oz / ¼ cup whole milk

2 large eggs

a pinch of salt

To Decorate

225 g / 8 oz / 1 cup unsalted
  butter, softened

180 g / 6 oz / 1 ½ cups icing
  (confectioners') sugar

1 tbsp boiling water

1 tsp strong instant espresso
  powder

55 g / 2 oz / ⅓ cup dark
  chocolate, melted

12

Makes

10

Preparation Time
(Minutes)

15–18

Cooking Time
(Minutes)

Method

- Preheat the oven to 180°C (160°C fan) / 350F / gas 4.

- Line a 12-hole cupcake tin with 12 cupcake cases.

- Beat together all the ingredients for the batter apart from the milk in a mixing bowl for 2 minutes until smooth and creamy.

- Add the milk and beat again for a further minute.

- Divide evenly between the paper cases before rapping the tin on a work surface to help settle the batter.

- Bake for 15–18 minutes until risen; test with a wooden toothpick, if it comes out clean, the cakes are done.

- Remove to a wire rack to cool as you prepare the buttercream.

- Beat the softened butter with the icing sugar in a mixing bowl until smooth.

- Mix together the espresso powder with the boiling water until smooth, then beat into the buttercream.

- Spoon into a piping bag fitted with a straight-sided nozzle and pipe a swirled mound on top of each cupcake.

- Pour the melted chocolate into a small piping bag and pipe small blobs on top of the buttercream, letting it set before serving.

Kiwi Cupcakes

Ingredients

110 g / 4 oz / ⅔ cup self-raising
  flour, sifted
110 g / 4 oz / ½ cup margarine,
  softened
110 g / 4 oz / ½ cup caster
  (superfine) sugar
1 tsp vanilla extract
2 large eggs
a pinch of salt

To Decorate

225 g / 8 oz / 1 cup unsalted butter,
  softened
180 g / 6 oz / 1 ½ cups icing
  (confectioners') sugar
a few drops of green food dye
2 kiwis, cut into 12 slices

12

Makes

10

Preparation Time
(Minutes)

15–18

Cooking Time
(Minutes)

Method

- Preheat the oven to 180°C (160°C fan) / 350F / gas 4.

- Line a 12-hole cupcake tin with 12 cupcake cases.

- Beat together all the ingredients for the batter in a mixing bowl for 2 minutes until smooth and creamy.

- Divide evenly between the paper cases before rapping the tin on a work surface to help settle the batter.

- Bake for 15–18 minutes until risen; test with a wooden toothpick, if it comes out clean, the cakes are done.

- Remove to a wire rack to cool as you prepare the buttercream.

- Beat the softened butter for 2 minutes until creamy and pale.

- Add the icing sugar and food dye and beat well.

- Spoon into a piping bag fitted with a petal tip before levelling the cupcakes using a serrated knife.

- Pipe buttercream leaves on top of the cupcakes before garnishing with a slice of kiwi fruit.

Macchiato Cupcakes

Ingredients

110 g / 4 oz / ⅔ cup self-raising
 flour, sifted

110 g / 4 oz / ½ cup margarine,
 softened

110 g / 4 oz / ½ cup caster
 (superfine) sugar

55 g / 2 oz / ⅓ cup cocoa powder

55 ml / 2 fl. oz / ¼ cup whole milk

2 large eggs

a pinch of salt

To Decorate

225 g / 8 oz / 1 cup unsalted butter,
 softened

180 g / 6 oz / 1 ½ cups icing
 (confectioners') sugar

1 tbsp cocoa powder

1 tbsp boiling water

1 tsp strong instant espresso powder

12 chocolate balls

12

Makes

10

Preparation Time
(Minutes)

15–18

Cooking Time
(Minutes)

Method

- Preheat the oven to 180°C (160°C fan) / 350F / gas 4.

- Line a 12-hole cupcake tin with 12 cupcake cases.

- Beat together all the ingredients for the batter apart from the milk in a mixing bowl for 2 minutes until smooth and creamy.

- Add the milk and beat again for a further minute.

- Divide evenly between the paper cases before rapping the tin on a work surface to help settle the batter.

- Bake for 15–18 minutes until risen; test with a wooden toothpick, if it comes out clean, the cakes are done.

- Remove to a wire rack to cool as you prepare the buttercream.

- Beat the softened butter with the icing sugar in a mixing bowl until smooth.

- Add the cocoa powder and boiling water and beat again.

- Spooning about one third of the buttercream into a piping bag fitted with a star-shaped nozzle.

- Spread the the tops of the cupcakes evenly with the remaining buttercream.

- Pipe a swirl of buttercream on top of the flat icing before garnishing the top with a chocolate balls.

Chocolate Mint Sweetie Cupcakes

Ingredients

110 g / 4 oz / ⅔ cup self-raising
flour, sifted

110 g / 4 oz / ½ cup margarine,
softened

110 g / 4 oz / ½ cup caster
(superfine) sugar

55 g / 2 oz / ⅓ cup cocoa powder

55 ml / 2 fl. oz / ¼ cup whole milk

2 large eggs

a pinch of salt

To Decorate

225 g / 8 oz / 1 cup unsalted butter,
softened

180 g / 6 oz / 1 ½ cups icing
(confectioners') sugar

1 tsp peppermint extract

a few drops of green food dye

12 wrapped mints

Makes

**Preparation Time
(Minutes)**

**Cooking Time
(Minutes)**

Method

- Preheat the oven to 180°C (160°C fan) / 350F / gas 4.

- Line a 12-hole cupcake tin with 12 cupcake cases.

- Beat together all the ingredients for the batter apart from the milk in a mixing bowl for 2 minutes until smooth and creamy.

- Add the milk and beat again for a further minute.

- Divide evenly between the paper cases before rapping the tin on a work surface to help settle the batter.

- Bake for 15–18 minutes until risen; test with a wooden toothpick, if it comes out clean, the cakes are done.

- Remove to a wire rack to cool as you prepare the buttercream.

- Beat the softened butter with the icing sugar in a mixing bowl until smooth.

- Add the peppermint extract and a few drops of green food dye until light green in dye.

- Spooning the buttercream into a piping bag fitted with a petal tip before piping ruffled mounds on top of the cupcakes.

- Garnish with a mint on top.

Chocolate Ball Mint Cupcakes

Ingredients

110 g / 4 oz / ⅔ cup self-raising flour, sifted

110 g / 4 oz / ½ cup margarine, softened

110 g / 4 oz / ½ cup caster (superfine) sugar

55 g / 2 oz / ⅓ cup cocoa powder

55 ml / 2 fl. oz / ¼ cup whole milk

2 large eggs

a pinch of salt

To Decorate

225 g / 8 oz / 1 cup unsalted butter, softened

180 g / 6 oz / 1 ½ cups icing (confectioners') sugar

2 tbsp cocoa powder

2 tbsp boiling water

½ tsp peppermint extract

125 ml / 4 ½ fl. oz / ½ cup double (heavy) cream

½ tsp vanilla extract

12 chocolate balls

12 sprigs of mint leaves

12

Makes

10

Preparation Time
(Minutes)

15–18

Cooking Time
(Minutes)

Method

- Preheat the oven to 180°C (160°C fan) / 350F / gas 4.

- Line a 12-hole cupcake tin with 12 cupcake cases.

- Beat together all the ingredients for the batter apart from the milk in a mixing bowl for 2 minutes until smooth and creamy.

- Add the milk and beat again for a further minute.

- Divide evenly between the paper cases before rapping the tin on a work surface to help settle the batter.

- Bake for 15–18 minutes until risen; test with a wooden toothpick, if it comes out clean, the cakes are done.

- Remove to a wire rack to cool as you prepare the buttercream.

- Beat the softened butter with the icing sugar in a mixing bowl until smooth.

- Add the cocoa powder, peppermint essence and boiling water and beat well until smooth.

- Spoon into a piping bag fitted with a small straight-sided nozzle.

- Pipe 6 tears around the edges of the cupcakes before whipping the cream with the vanilla extract.

- Spoon a little cream in the centre before garnishing with a chocolate ball and a sprig of mint leaves.

Novelty

Gingerbread Man Cupcakes

Ingredients

110 g / 4 oz / ⅔ cup self-raising
flour, sifted

110 g / 4 oz / ½ cup caster
(superfine) sugar

110 g / 4 oz / ½ cup butter, softened

2 large eggs

1 lemon, juiced and zest finely
grated

To Decorate

100 g / 3 ½ oz / ½ cup butter, softened

200 g / 7 oz / 2 cups icing
(confectioners') sugar

½ lemon, juiced and zest finely grated

yellow, brown and red food dye

110 g / 4 oz / 1 cup ready to roll fondant
icing

12

Makes

70

Preparation Time
(Minutes)

15–20

Cooking Time
(Minutes)

Method

- Preheat the oven to 190°C (170°C
  fan) / 375F / gas 5 and line a 12-
  hole cupcake tin with paper cases.

- Combine the flour, sugar, butter,
  eggs and lemon juice and zest
  in a bowl and whisk together for
  2 minutes or until smooth. Divide
  the mixture between the cases,
  then transfer the tin to the oven
  and bake for 15–20 minutes.

- Test with a wooden toothpick, if
  it comes out clean, the cakes are
  done. Transfer the cakes to a wire
  rack and leave to cool completely.

- Beat the butter until smooth, then
  gradually whisk in the icing sugar,
  lemon juice and zest and a few
  drops of yellow food dye.

- Spoon the mixture into a piping
  bag, fitted with a large star nozzle
  and pipe a swirl of buttercream
  on top of each cake.

- Dye the fondant icing brown and
  roll it out on a work surface that has
  been lightly dusted with icing sugar.

- Use a small gingerbread man cutter
  to cut out 12 gingerbread men.

- Use the end of a round piping
  nozzle to make the imprint of
  buttons down their chests.

- Use a small paint brush to paint
  on their shoes with some brown
  food dye.

- Add the facial features with a plain
  piping nozzle, pressing it in at an
  angle to make a semi-circle for
  the mouth.

- Paint on some gloves using a
  small paint brush and some
  red food dye.

- Transfer each gingerbread
  man to the top of a cake.

Crown Cupcakes

Ingredients

110 g / 4 oz / ⅔ cup self-raising
  flour, sifted

110 g / 4 oz / ½ cup caster
  (superfine) sugar

110 g / 4 oz / ½ cup butter, softened

2 large eggs

1 lemon, juiced and zest finely
  grated

To Decorate

100 g / 3 ½ oz / ½ cup butter, softened

200 g / 7 oz / 2 cups icing
  (confectioners') sugar

½ lemon, juiced and zest finely grated

yellow food dye

400 g / 7 oz / 1 cup ready to roll
  fondant icing

edible silver balls

12

Makes

70

Preparation Time
(Minutes)

15–20

Cooking Time
(Minutes)

Methods

- Preheat the oven to 190°C (170°C fan) / 375F / gas 5 and line a 12-hole cupcake tin with paper cases.

- Combine the flour, sugar, butter, eggs and lemon juice and zest in a bowl and whisk together for 2 minutes or until smooth. Divide the mixture between the cases, then transfer the tin to the oven and bake for 15–20 minutes.

- Test with a wooden toothpick, if it comes out clean, the cakes are done. Transfer the cakes to a wire rack and leave to cool completely.

- Beat the butter until smooth, then gradually whisk in the icing sugar, lemon juice and zest and a few drops of yellow food dye.

- Spoon the mixture into a piping bag, fitted with a large plain nozzle and pipe a swirl of buttercream on top of each cake.

- Dye the fondant icing yellow and roll it out on a work surface that has been lightly dusted with icing sugar.

- Cut it into 12 ribbons 2.5 cm (1 in) thick, then cut a zigzag into one edge with a sharp knife.

- Make a dent below the centre of each pint with a small ball tool.

- Paint a little edible flower glue into each indentation.

- Press a silver ball into each indentation and wait for a few minutes for the glue to work.

- Fold each strip round to form a crown and press them lightly into the top of the buttercream to hold the shape.

Baby Boots Cupcakes

Ingredients

110 g / 4 oz / ⅔ cup self-raising
flour, sifted

110 g / 4 oz / ½ cup caster
(superfine) sugar

110 g / 4 oz / ½ cup butter, softened

2 large eggs

1 tsp vanilla extract

To Decorate

400 g / 14 oz ready to roll fondant icing

blue food dye

icing (confectioners') sugar for dusting

12

Makes

75

Preparation Time
(Minutes)

15–20

Cooking Time
(Minutes)

Method

- Preheat the oven to 190°C (170°C fan) / 375F / gas 5 and line a 12-hole cupcake tin with paper cases.

- Combine the flour, sugar, butter, eggs and vanilla extract in a bowl and whisk together for 2 minutes. Divide the mixture between the cases, then transfer the tin to the oven and bake for 15–20 minutes.

- Test with a wooden toothpick, if it comes out clean, the cakes are done. Transfer the cakes to a wire rack and leave to cool completely.

- Dye half of the fondant icing bright blue. Dust the work surface with icing sugar and roll out the blue icing. Use a cookie cutter the same diameter as the top of the cakes to cut out 12 circles. Place on the cakes with a dab of water.

- Reserve a small piece of the white fondant icing for the flowers and dye the rest pale blue.

- Roll the pale blue icing into 12 balls and reserve.

- Shape the remaining two thirds of each ball into pear shapes.

- Dip a ball tool into icing sugar, then make a hollow in the thinner end of each pear shape.

- Roll the remaining third of each ball into a thick disk and use a cocktail stick to make indentations round the outside.

- Attach each disk to the top of a boot with a little water and hollow the insides with a smaller ball tool.

- Use the end of a small star nozzle to make an imprint on the front of each boot.

- Roll out the reserved white icing and cut out 12 small flowers with a plunger cutter and attach to the top of the cakes with a dab of water.

- Use some of the bright blue icing off-cuts to make the flower centres.

- Attach a boot to the top of each cake with a drop of water.

Beach Shoes Cupcakes

Ingredients

110 g / 4 oz / ⅔ cup self-raising
flour, sifted

110 g / 4 oz / ½ cup caster
(superfine) sugar

110 g / 4 oz / ½ cup butter, softened

2 large eggs

2 tbsp unsweetened cocoa powder

To Decorate

110 g / 4 oz / ½ cup light brown sugar

110 g / 4 oz ready to roll fondant icing

red food dye

12

Makes

50

Preparation Time
(Minutes)

15–20

Cooking Time
(Minutes)

Methods

• Preheat the oven to 190°C (170°C fan) / 375F / gas 5 and line a 12-hole cupcake tin with paper cases.

• Combine the flour, sugar, butter, eggs and cocoa powder in a bowl and whisk together for 2 minutes or until smooth. Divide the mixture between the cases, then transfer the tin to the oven and bake for 15–20 minutes.

• Test with a wooden toothpick, if it comes out clean, the cakes are done. Transfer the cakes to a wire rack and leave to cool completely.

• Top each cake with a thick layer of brown sugar 'sand' and make ripples in it with the spoon handle.

• Reserve 1 quarter of the fondant icing and dye the rest red.

• Brush the inside of a silicone flip-flop mould with icing sugar.

• Press a small amount of the white icing into the strap details inside the mould, making sure the top is flush with the design.

• Press a ball of red icing into each of the mould's indents and press down firmly to flatten.

• Turn the mould upside down and peel it away to reveal the icing flip-flops.

• Position 2 flip flops on top of each cake.

Black and White Cupcakes

Ingredients

110 g / 4 oz / ⅔ cup self-raising flour, sifted

110 g / 4 oz / ½ cup caster (superfine) sugar

110 g / 4 oz / ½ cup butter, softened

2 large eggs

1 tsp vanilla extract

To Decorate

100 g / 3 ½ oz / ½ cup butter, softened

200 g / 7 oz / 2 cups icing (confectioners') sugar

½ tsp vanilla extract

200 g / 7 oz ready to roll fondant icing

black food dye

12

Makes

60

Preparation Time
(Minutes)

15–20

Cooking Time
(Minutes)

Methods

- Preheat the oven to 190°C (170°C fan) / 375F / gas 5 and line a 12-hole cupcake tin with paper cases.

- Combine the flour, sugar, butter, eggs and vanilla extract in a bowl and whisk together for 2 minutes or until smooth. Divide the mixture between the cases, then transfer the tin to the oven and bake for 15–20 minutes.

- Test with a wooden toothpick, if it comes out clean, the cakes are done. Transfer the cakes to a wire rack and leave to cool completely.

- Beat the butter until smooth, then gradually whisk in the icing sugar and vanilla extract. Spread the buttercream on top of the cakes, levelling the top with a palette knife.

- Dust the work surface lightly with icing sugar and roll out two thirds of the fondant icing.

- Use a cookie cutter the same diameter as the top of the cakes to cut out 12 circles.

- Attach an icing circle to the top of each cake.

- Dye the remaining icing black, divide it in half and roll it out into 2 long strips on the work surface.

- Slice one piece into thin slices with a pizza wheel.

- Cut out thin circles from the other piece with a small plunger cutter.

- Lay 4 strips of black icing across the top of each cake, securing with a dab of water.

- Cut off the edges of the black icing strips with a sharp knife.

- Add a row of black icing dots between 2 of the strips of black icing, securing with a little water as before.

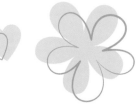

Camper-van Cupcakes

Ingredients

110 g / 4 oz / ⅔ cup self-raising flour, sifted

110 g / 4 oz / ½ cup caster (superfine) sugar

110 g / 4 oz / ½ cup butter, softened

2 large eggs

1 lemon, juiced and zest finely grated

To Decorate

400 g / 14 oz ready to roll fondant icing

blue, orange, yellow, red and black food dye

icing (confectioners') sugar for dusting

12

Makes

90

Preparation Time (Minutes)

15–20

Cooking Time (Minutes)

Methods

- Preheat the oven to 190°C (170°C fan) / 375F / gas 5 and line a 12-hole cupcake tin with paper cases.

- Combine the flour, sugar, butter, eggs and lemon juice and zest in a bowl and whisk together for 2 minutes or until smooth. Divide the mixture between the cases, then transfer the tin to the oven and bake for 15–20 minutes.

- Test with a wooden toothpick, if it comes out clean, the cakes are done. Transfer the cakes to a wire rack and leave to cool completely.

- Dye half of the fondant icing blue. Dust the work surface lightly with icing sugar and roll out the blue icing. Use a cookie cutter the same diameter as the top of the cakes to cut out 12 circles then attach them to the top of the cakes with a dab of water.

- Use the same cookie cutter to gauge the correct size for the

camper van and make a template out of strong card.

- Dye half of the remaining icing orange and roll it out then use the template to help you cut out 12 van shapes with a scalpel.

- Roll out the white icing and cut out 12 more van shapes.

- Stack the white shapes on top of the orange shapes and cut a 'v' through each.

- Assemble the vans on top of the cakes, using the white tops and the orange bottoms, attaching with a dab of water.

- Use a round plunger cutter to cut circles out of the orange icing off-cuts and attach them to the cakes with a dab of water.

- Dye half of the white icing off-cuts yellow and use a plunger cutter to make the headlights and indicators.

Funky Toadstool Cupcakes

Ingredients

40 g / 1 ½ oz / ¼ cup butter,
    unsalted, softened
140 g / 5 oz / ½ cup caster
    (superfine) sugar
100 g / 3 ½ oz / 1 cup plain
    (all purpose) flour
20 g / 1 oz cocoa powder
1 ½ tsp baking powder
1 egg
50 ml / 2 fl. oz / ¼ cup cream liqueur
80 ml / 3 fl.oz / ¼ cup whole milk

To Decorate

125 g / 4 ½ oz / ½ cup butter
500 g /18 oz / 4 cups icing sugar
45 ml / 2 fl. oz / ¼ cup Baileys
1 tbsp. milk
Iced mushroom candies

10

Makes

20

Preparation Time
(Minutes)

15–20

Cooking Time
(Minutes)

Methods

- Preheat the oven to 170°C (150°C fan) / 325F / gas 3 and line a cupcake tin with paper cases.

- Place the butter, sugar, flour, cocoa powder and baking powder into a large bowl and using a hand held or freestanding electric mixer, slowly mix together until it resembles breadcrumbs.

- Mix together the egg, Irish cream liqueur and milk in a jug then gradually add to the bowl and mix thoroughly.

- Spoon some cupcake mix into each paper case.

- Bake, for 15–20 minutes. Test with a wooden toothpick, if it comes out clean, the cakes are done.

- Place on a wire rack to cool.

- To make the buttercream beat the butter with a whisk until soft and gradually beat in the icing sugar, milk and Irish cream liqueur.

- Pipe buttercream and place mushrooms.

Getting Piggy Cupcakes

Ingredients

110 g / 4 oz / ⅔ cup self-raising flour, sifted

110 g / 4 oz / ½ cup margarine, softened

110 g / 4 oz / ½ cup caster (superfine) sugar

1 tsp vanilla extract

2 large eggs

a pinch of salt

To Decorate

175 g / 6 oz / ¾ cup unsalted butter, softened

125 g / 4 ½ oz / 1 cup icing (confectioner's) sugar

a few drops of red food dye

12 jelly pigs (use pig face chocolates if not available)

12 strawberry truffles

50 g / 2 oz / ¼ cup pink sugarpaste

12

Makes

10

Preparation Time (Minutes)

20

Cooking Time (Minutes)

Methods

- Preheat the oven to 180°C (160°C fan) / 350F / gas 4.

- Line a 12-hole cupcake tin with 12 cupcake cases.

- Beat together all the ingredients for the batter in a mixing bowl for 2 minutes until smooth and creamy.

- Divide evenly between the paper cases before rapping the tin on a work surface to help settle the batter.

- Bake for 15–18 minutes until risen; test with a wooden toothpick, if it comes out clean, the cakes are done.

- Remove to a wire rack to cool as you prepare the buttercream.

- Beat the softened butter in a mixing bowl for 3–4 minutes until pale.

- Add the icing sugar and beat well before beating in the food dye until you reach a light pink dye.

- Spread evenly on top of the cupcakes using a small palette knife, reserving about a tablespoon of icing.

- Roll small tacks of sugarpaste into trotters and shape some more into tails before attaching in place on the truffles.

- Spread the backs of the jelly pigs with icing before attaching to the truffles.

- Sit on top of the cupcakes before serving.

Blueberry Smile Cupcakes

Ingredients

110 g / 4 oz / ⅔ cup self-raising
  flour, sifted

110 g / 4 oz / ½ cup margarine,
  softened

110 g / 4 oz / ½ cup caster
  (superfine) sugar

1 tsp vanilla extract

2 large eggs

a pinch of salt

To Decorate

225 g / 8 oz / 1 cup unsalted butter,
  softened

180 g / 6 oz / 1 ½ cups icing
  (confectioners') sugar

1 tbsp lemon juice

a few drops of blue food dye

100 g / 3 ½ oz / 1 cup blueberries

12

Makes

10

Preparation Time
(Minutes)

15–18

Cooking Time
(Minutes)

Methods

- Preheat the oven to 180°C (160°C fan) / 350F / gas 4.

- Line a 12-hole cupcake tin with 12 cupcake cases.

- Beat together all the ingredients for the batter in a mixing bowl for 2 minutes until smooth and creamy.

- Divide evenly between the paper cases before rapping the tin on a work surface to help settle the batter.

- Bake for 15–18 minutes until risen; test with a wooden toothpick, if it comes out clean, the cakes are done.

- Remove to a wire rack to cool as you prepare the buttercream.

- Beat the butter with the icing sugar, lemon juice and drops of food dye until you have an even light purple buttercream.

- Spread the tops of the cupcake evenly with the buttercream before positioning 2 blueberries as eyes.

- Use a knife to draw smiles in the icing.

Orange Jelly-ring Cupcakes

Ingredients

110 g / 4 oz / ⅔ cup self-raising
flour, sifted

110 g / 4 oz / ½ cup margarine,
softened

110 g / 4 oz / ½ cup caster
(superfine) sugar

1 tsp orange flower water

2 large eggs

a pinch of salt

To Decorate

225 g / 8 oz / 1 cup unsalted butter,
softened

180 g / 6 oz / 1 ½ cups icing
(confectioners') sugar

1 tsp orange flower water

36 orange jelly beans

12 jelly rings

12

Makes

10

Preparation Time
(Minutes)

15–18

Cooking Time
(Minutes)

Methods

- Preheat the oven to 180°C (160°C fan) / 350F / gas 4.

- Line a 12-hole cupcake tin with 12 cupcake cases.

- Beat together all the ingredients for the batter in a mixing bowl for 2 minutes until smooth and creamy.

- Divide evenly between the paper cases before rapping the tin on a work surface to help settle the batter.

- Bake for 15–18 minutes until risen; test with a wooden toothpick, if it comes out clean, the cakes are done.

- Remove to a wire rack to cool as you prepare the orange buttercream.

- Beat the softened butter for 2 minutes until creamy and pale.

- Add the icing sugar and orange extract and beat again until smooth.

- Spoon into a piping bag fitted with a straight-sided nozzle before piping spiral swirls on top.

- Garnish with a jelly ring on top and orange jelly beans on the sides.

Chocolate Cola Bottle Cupcakes

Ingredients

110 g / 4 oz / ⅔ cup self-raising flour, sifted

110 g / 4 oz / ½ cup margarine, softened

110 g / 4 oz / ½ cup caster (superfine) sugar

55 g / 2 oz / ⅓ cup cocoa powder

55 ml / 2 fl. oz / ¼ cup whole milk

2 large eggs

a pinch of salt

To Decorate

225 g / 8 oz / 1 cup unsalted butter, softened

180 g / 6 oz / 1 ½ cups icing (confectioners') sugar

2 tbsp cocoa powder

2 tbsp boiling water

125 ml / 4 ½ fl. oz / ½ cup double heavy cream

½ tsp vanilla extract

12 cola bottle sweets

12 red straws

12

Makes

10

Preparation Time (Minutes)

15–18

Cooking Time (Minutes)

Methods

- Preheat the oven to 180°C (160°C fan) / 350F / gas 4.

- Line a 12-hole cupcake tin with 12 cupcake cases.

- Beat together all the ingredients for the batter apart from the milk in a mixing bowl for 2 minutes until smooth and creamy.

- Add the milk and beat again for a further minute.

- Divide evenly between the paper cases before rapping the tin on a work surface to help settle the batter.

- Bake for 15–18 minutes until risen; test with a wooden toothpick, if it comes out clean, the cakes are done.

- Remove to a wire rack to cool as you prepare the buttercream.

- Beat the softened butter with the icing sugar in a mixing bowl until smooth.

- Add the cocoa powder and boiling water and beat well until smooth.

- Spoon into a piping bag fitted with a straight-sided nozzle and pipe spiral swirls on top of the cupcakes.

- Whip the cream with the vanilla extract and spoon into a piping bag fitted with a star-shaped nozzle.

- Pipe stars of cream on top of the buttercream before decoratinggarnishing with a cola bottle and a straw.

130

Mint Cookie Cupcakes

Ingredients

110 g / 4 oz / ⅔ cup self-raising
    flour, sifted

110 g / 4 oz / ½ cup margarine,
    softened

110 g / 4 oz / ½ cup caster
    (superfine) sugar

55 g / 2 oz / ⅓ cup cocoa powder

55 ml / 2 fl. oz / ¼ cup whole milk

2 large eggs

a pinch of salt

To Decorate

225 g / 8 oz / 1 cup unsalted butter,
    softened

180 g / 6 oz / 1 ½ cups icing
    (confectioner's) sugar

1 tsp peppermint extract

a few drops of green food dye

6 bourbon biscuits, chopped

12

Makes

10

**Preparation Time
(Minutes)**

15–18

**Cooking Time
(Minutes)**

Methods

- Preheat the oven to 180°C (160°C fan) / 350F / gas 4.

- Line a 12-hole cupcake tin with 12 cupcake cases.

- Beat together all the ingredients for the batter apart from the milk in a mixing bowl for 2 minutes until smooth and creamy.

- Add the milk and beat again for a further minute.

- Divide evenly between the paper cases before rapping the tin on a work surface to help settle the batter.

- Bake for 15–18 minutes until risen; test with a wooden toothpick, if it comes out clean, the cakes are done.

- Remove to a wire rack to cool as you prepare the buttercream.

- Beat the softened butter with the icing sugar in a mixing bowl until smooth.

- Add the peppermint extract and a few drops of green food dye until light green in dye.

- Spread the buttercream on top of the cupcakes, creating a mound.

- Garnish with the bourbon biscuits before serving.

Mint Julep Cupcakes

Ingredients

110 g / 4 oz / ⅔ cup self-raising
  flour, sifted

110 g / 4 oz / ½ cup margarine,
  softened

110 g / 4 oz / ½ cup caster
  (superfine) sugar

1 tsp vanilla extract

2 large eggs

a pinch of salt

To Decorate

300 g / 10 ½ oz / 1 ⅓ cups unsalted
  butter, softened

250 g / 9 oz / 2 cups icing
  (confectioners') sugar

1 tsp vanilla extract

1 tsp peppermint extract

a few drops of green food dye

12 red jelly beans

12 small mint leaves

12 red straws

12

Makes

10

Preparation Time
(Minutes)

15–18

Cooking Time
(Minutes)

Methods

- Preheat the oven to 180°C (160°C fan) / 350F / gas 4.

- Line a 12-hole cupcake tin with 12 cupcake cases.

- Beat together all the ingredients for the batter in a mixing bowl for 2 minutes until smooth and creamy.

- Divide evenly between the paper cases before rapping the tin on a work surface to help settle the batter.

- Bake for 15–18 minutes until risen; test with a wooden toothpick, if it comes out clean, the cakes are done.

- Remove to a wire rack to cool as you prepare the buttercream.

- Beat the softened butter for 2–3 minutes until creamy and pale.

- Add the icing sugar and beat again until smooth before spooning ⅔ of the buttercream into another bowl.

- Add the peppermint extract and a few drops of green food dye into the second bowl and add the vanilla extract to the first bowl.

- Beat the ingredients in both bowls well before spooning the mint buttercream into a piping bag fitted with a petal tip.

- Level the tops of the cupcakes before spreading their tops with the vanilla buttercream.

- Pipe a ruffled swirl of mint buttercream on top and garnish with a jelly bean, mint leaf and straw.

Lime and Ginger Jelly Bean Cupcakes

Ingredients

110 g / 4 oz / ⅔ cup self-raising
   flour, sifted
110 g / 4 oz / ½ cup margarine,
   softened
110 g / 4 oz / ½ cup caster
   (superfine) sugar
1 tsp vanilla extract
1 tsp ground ginger
2 large eggs
a pinch of salt

To Decorate

225 g / 8 oz / 1 cup unsalted butter,
   softened
180 g / 6 oz / 1 ½ cups icing
   (confectioners') sugar
2 tbsp lime juice
1 tbsp ginger cordial
60 assorted jelly beans

12

Makes

10

Preparation Time
(Minutes)

15–18

Cooking Time
(Minutes)

Methods

- Preheat the oven to 180°C (160°C fan) / 350F / gas 4.

- Line a 12-hole cupcake tin with 12 cupcake cases.

- Beat together all the ingredients for the batter in a mixing bowl for 2 minutes until smooth and creamy.

- Divide evenly between the paper cases before rapping the tin on a work surface to help settle the batter.

- Bake for 15–18 minutes until risen; test with a wooden toothpick, if it comes out clean, the cakes are done.

- Remove to a wire rack to cool as you prepare the buttercream.

- Beat the softened butter for 2 minutes until creamy and pale.

- Add the icing sugar, lime juice and ginger cordials and beat well until smooth.

- Spoon into a piping bag fitted with a star-shaped nozzle before levelling the cupcakes.

- Pipe ice-cream swirls of buttercream on top before garnishing each with 5 jelly beans.

Chocolate, Raspberry and Kiwi Cupcakes

Ingredients

110 g / 4 oz / ⅔ cup self-raising flour, sifted

110 g / 4 oz / ½ cup margarine, softened

110 g / 4 oz / ½ cup caster (superfine) sugar

1 tsp vanilla extract

2 large eggs

a pinch of salt

To Decorate

250 ml / 9 fl. oz / 1 cup double (heavy) cream

65 g / 2 ½ oz / ½ cup icing (confectioners') sugar

1 tsp vanilla extract

12 raspberries

12 white and dark chocolate cigarillos

12 sprigs of mint leaves

1 kiwi fruit, cut into 12 semi-circles

12

Makes

10

Preparation Time (Minutes)

15-18

Cooking Time (Minutes)

Methods

- Preheat the oven to 180°C (160°C fan) / 350F / gas 4.

- Line a 12-hole cupcake tin with 12 cupcake cases.

- Beat together all the ingredients for the batter in a mixing bowl for 2 minutes until smooth and creamy.

- Divide evenly between the paper cases before rapping the tin on a work surface to help settle the batter.

- Bake for 15–18 minutes until risen; test with a wooden toothpick, if it comes out clean, the cakes are done.

- Remove to a wire rack to cool as you prepare the buttercream.

- Whip the cream with the icing sugar and vanilla extract until almost clotted.

- Spoon on top of the cupcakes and garnish with the fruit and cigarillos.

Jam-filled Biscuit Cupcakes

Ingredients

110 g / 4 oz / ⅔ cup self-raising
   flour, sifted

110 g / 4 oz / ½ cup margarine,
   softened

110 g / 4 oz / ½ cup caster
   (superfine) sugar

1 tsp vanilla extract

2 large eggs

a pinch of salt

To Decorate

175 g / 6 oz / ¾ cup unsalted butter,
   softened

125 g / 4 ½ oz / 1 cup icing
   (confectioners') sugar

1 tsp vanilla extract

12 jam filled biscuits

12 strawberry belts, halved
   lengthways and cut into 3cm (1
   in) strips

12

Makes

10

Preparation Time
(Minutes)

15–18

Cooking Time
(Minutes)

Methods

- Preheat the oven to 180°C (160°C fan) / 350F / gas 4.

- Line a 12-hole cupcake tin with 12 cupcake cases.

- Beat together all the ingredients for the batter in a mixing bowl for 2 minutes until smooth and creamy.

- Divide evenly between the paper cases before rapping the tin on a work surface to help settle the batter.

- Bake for 15–18 minutes until risen; test with a wooden toothpick, if it comes out clean, the cakes are done.

- Remove to a wire rack to cool as you prepare the buttercream.

- Beat the softened butter for 2 minutes until creamy and pale.

- Add the icing sugar and vanilla extract and beat well until smooth.

- Spread the icing on top of the cupcakes until level.

- Fold the belts over so that the ends meet before attaching to the buttercream around the perimeter,

- Place a jam-filled biscuit in the centre of each cupcake before serving.

Dove Cupcakes

Ingredients

110 g / 4 oz / ⅔ cup self-raising
flour, sifted

110 g / 4 oz / ½ cup caster
(superfine) sugar

110 g / 4 oz / ½ cup butter, softened

2 large eggs

1 tsp vanilla extract

To Decorate

100 g / 3 ½ oz / ½ cup butter, softened

200 g / 7 oz / 2 cups icing
(confectioners') sugar

½ tsp vanilla extract

200 g / 7 oz ½ cup ready to roll fondant
icing

ivory food dye

12

Makes

60

Preparation Time
(Minutes)

15–20

Cooking Time
(Minutes)

Methods

- Preheat the oven to 190°C (170°C fan) / 375F / gas 5 and line a 12-hole cupcake tin with paper cases.

- Combine the flour, sugar, butter, eggs and vanilla extract in a bowl and whisk together for 2 minutes or until smooth. Divide the mixture between the cases, then transfer the tin to the oven and bake for 15–20 minutes.

- Test with a wooden toothpick, if it comes out clean, the cakes are done. Transfer the cakes to a wire rack and leave to cool completely.

- Beat the butter until smooth, then gradually whisk in the icing sugar and vanilla extract. Spread the buttercream on top of the cakes, levelling the top with a palette knife.

- Dust the work surface lightly with icing sugar and roll out three quarters of the fondant icing.

- Use a cookie cutter the same diameter as the top of the cakes to cut out 12 circles.

- Attach an icing circle to the top of each cake.

- Dye the rest of the icing a pale ivory dye.

- Dust the inside of a dove-shaped mould with a little icing sugar.

- Press a small ball of icing into the mould, making sure it goes into every corner.

- Carefully turn out the dove onto the work surface and repeat the process to make 12 doves in total.

- Attach a dove to the top of each cake with a dab of water.

Pink Guitar Cupcakes

Ingredients

110 g / 4 oz / ⅔ cup self-raising flour, sifted

110 g / 4 oz / ½ cup margarine, softened

110 g / 4 oz / ½ cup caster (superfine) sugar

1 tsp vanilla extract

2 large eggs

a pinch of salt

To Decorate

225 g / 8 oz / 1 cup ready-made white fondant icing

30 g / 1 oz / 2 tbsp apricot jam (jelly)

1 tbsp icing (confectioner's) sugar, for dusting

96 white candy necklace beads

12 pink fondant guitars

12

Makes

10

Preparation Time (Minutes)

15–18

Cooking Time (Minutes)

Methods

- Preheat the oven to 180°C (160°C fan) / 350F / gas 4.

- Line a 12-hole cupcake tin with 12 cupcake cases.

- Beat together all the ingredients for the batter in a mixing bowl for 2 minutes until smooth and creamy.

- Divide evenly between the paper cases before rapping the tin on a work surface to help settle the batter.

- Bake for 15–18 minutes until risen; test with a wooden toothpick, if it comes out clean, the cakes are done.

- Remove to a wire rack to cool as you prepare the buttercream.

- Roll the fondant icing on a surface dusted with icing sugar.

- Use a fluted cookie cutter to stamp out 12 rounds of icing slightly larger than the diameter of the cupcakes.

- Brush the undersides of the icing rounds with apricot jam before securing on top of the cupcakes.

- Lightly press the guitars and candy necklace beads into the icing before serving.

Owl Cupcakes

Ingredients

110 g / 4 oz / ⅔ cup self-raising flour, sifted

110 g / 4 oz / ½ cup caster (superfine) sugar

110 g / 4 oz / ½ cup butter, softened

2 large eggs

1 lemon, juiced and zest finely grated

To Decorate

400 g / 14 oz ready to roll fondant icing

blue, brown, red, purple and yellow food dye

icing (confectioners') sugar for dusting

Methods

- Preheat the oven to 190°C (170° fan) / 375F / gas 5 and line a 12-hole cupcake tin with paper cases.

- Combine the flour, sugar, butter, eggs and lemon juice and zest in a bowl and whisk together for 2 minutes or until smooth. Divide the mixture between the cases, then transfer the tin to the oven and bake for 15–20 minutes.

- Test with a wooden toothpick, if it comes out clean, the cakes are done. Transfer the cakes to a wire rack and leave to cool completely.

- Dye half of the fondant icing pale blue. Dust the work surface lightly with icing sugar and roll out the blue icing.

- Use a cookie cutter the same diameter as the top of the cakes to cut out 12 circles then attach them to the top of the cakes with a dab of water.

- Divide the rest of the icing into 3 pieces. Dye one piece brown and

one piece red. Divide the remaining piece in half and dye one piece yellow and the other purple.

- Roll out the brown icing and cut it into 12 branch shapes with a pizza wheel.

- Attach the branches to the cakes with a dab of water.

- Roll out the red icing and cut out 12 circles 5 cm (2 in) in diameter.

- Cut the top off each circle to make a flat edge and attach them to the cakes with the flat edge at the top.

- Cut 24 small triangles out of the red trimmings to make the ears and attach them to the cakes.

- Roll out the yellow icing and use a small round plunger cutter to cut out 12 pairs of eyes. Attach them to the cake with a little water.

- Use the purple icing to make smaller circles for the pupils of the eyes.

12

Makes

90

Preparation Time (Minutes)

15–20

Cooking Time (Minutes)

Fondant Cherry Cupcakes

Ingredients

110 g / 4 oz / ⅔ cup self-raising flour,
  sifted
110 g / 4 oz / ½ cup caster
  (superfine) sugar
110 g / 4 oz / ½ cup butter, softened
2 large eggs
2 tbsp unsweetened cocoa powder

To Decorate

100 g / 3 ½ oz / ½ cup butter, softened
200 g / 7 oz / 2 cups icing
  (confectioners') sugar
½ tsp vanilla extract
110 g / 4 oz ready to roll fondant icing
red and green food dye

12

Makes

60

Preparation Time
(Minutes)

15–20

Cooking Time
(Minutes)

Methods

- Preheat the oven to 190°C (170°C fan) / 375F / gas 5 and line a 12-hole cupcake tin with paper cases.

- Combine the flour, sugar, butter, eggs and cocoa powder in a bowl and whisk together for 2 minutes or until smooth. Divide the mixture between the cases, then transfer the tin to the oven and bake for 15–20 minutes.

- Test with a wooden toothpick, if it comes out clean, the cakes are done. Transfer the cakes to a wire rack and leave to cool completely.

- Beat the butter until smooth, then gradually whisk in the icing sugar and vanilla extract.

- Spoon the mixture into a piping

bag, fitted with a large star nozzle and pipe a swirl of buttercream on top of each cake.

- Dye three quarters of the fondant icing red and roll it into 12 balls.

- Make an indentation in the top of each one with a veining tool.

- Dye the rest of the icing green and roll it into a long thin sausage.

- Cut the green icing into 12 cherry stalks.

- Sit a cherry on top of each cake and attach the stalks with a dab of water.

Minty Heart Cupcakes

Ingredients

110 g / 4 oz / ⅔ cup self-raising
   flour, sifted

110 g / 4 oz / ½ cup margarine,
   softened

110 g / 4 oz / ½ cup caster
   (superfine) sugar

1 tsp vanilla extract

2 large eggs

a pinch of salt

To Decorate

225 g / 8 oz / 1 cup unsalted butter,
   softened

180 g / 6 oz / 1 ½ cups icing
   (confectioners') sugar

1 tsp peppermint extract

a few drops of green food dye

12 jelly hearts

12 sprigs of mint leaves

12

Makes

10

Preparation Time
(Minutes)

15–18

Cooking Time
(Minutes)

Methods

- Preheat the oven to 180°C (160°C fan) / 350F / gas 4.

- Line a 12-hole cupcake tin with 12 cupcake cases.

- Beat together all the ingredients for the batter in a mixing bowl for 2 minutes until smooth and creamy.

- Divide evenly between the paper cases before rapping the tin on a work surface to help settle the batter.

- Bake for 15–18 minutes until risen; test with a wooden toothpick, if it comes out clean, the cakes are done.

- Remove to a wire rack to cool as you prepare the buttercream.

- Beat the softened butter for 2 minutes until creamy and pale.

- Add the icing sugar, peppermint extract and green food dye, beating well until uniformly light green.

- Spoon into a piping bag fitted with a petal tip before piping ruffled mounds on top of the cupcakes.

- Garnish with jelly hearts and sprigs of mint leaves.

Pearls Cupcakes

Ingredients

110 g / 4 oz / ⅔ cup self-raising flour, sifted

110 g / 4 oz / ½ cup caster (superfine) sugar

110 g / 4 oz / ½ cup butter, softened

2 large eggs

1 lemon, juiced and zest finely grated

To Decorate

400 g / 14 oz / 1 cups ready to roll fondant icing

ivory food dye

icing (confectioners') sugar for dusting

pearlescent dusting powder

12

Makes

90

Preparation Time (Minutes)

15–20

Cooking Time (Minutes)

Methods

- Preheat the oven to 190°C (170°C fan) / 375F / gas 5 and line a 12-hole cupcake tin with paper cases.

- Combine the flour, sugar, butter, eggs and lemon juice and zest in a bowl and whisk together for 2 minutes or until smooth. Divide the mixture between the cases, then transfer the tin to the oven and bake for 15–20 minutes.

- Test with a wooden toothpick, if it comes out clean, the cakes are done. Transfer the cakes to a wire rack and leave to cool completely.

- Dust the work surface lightly with icing sugar and roll out two thirds of the fondant icing, then use a scalloped edge cookie cutter the same diameter as the top of the cakes to cut out 12 circles.

- Attach an icing circle to the top of each cake with a dab of water and reserve the off-cuts.

- Dye the rest of the icing ivory and roll it out. Use a smaller scalloped

edge cookie cutter to cut out 12 circles and attach each one to the top of a cake with a dab of water.

- Roll the white icing off-cuts into a 5 mm diameter sausage and cut it into 5mm lengths. Roll each piece of icing into a smooth ball with your hands and transfer to a small bowl.

- Sprinkle in some pearlescent dusting powder.

- Swirl the bowl to coat the icing balls in the powder.

- Brush the rim of the ivory icing circles with a little water.

- Stick the icing pearls to the top of the cakes in a ring where the icing is wet.

- Add a single pearl to the centre of each cake, using water to attach as before.

Pink Champagne Cupcakes

Ingredients

110 g / 4 oz / ⅔ cup self-raising flour, sifted

110 g / 4 oz / ½ cup caster (superfine) sugar

110 g / 4 oz / ½ cup butter, softened

2 large eggs

1 tsp vanilla extract

To Decorate

100 g / 3 ½ oz / ½ cup butter, softened

200 g / 7 oz / 2 cups icing (confectioners') sugar

½ tsp vanilla extract

110 g / 4 oz ready to roll fondant icing

pink food dye

edible glitter

12

Makes

70

Preparation Time (Minutes)

15–20

Cooking Time (Minutes)

Methods

- Preheat the oven to 190°C (170°C fan) / 375F / gas 5 and line a 12-hole cupcake tin with paper cases.

- Combine the flour, sugar, butter, eggs and vanilla extract in a bowl and whisk together for 2 minutes or until smooth. Divide the mixture between the cases, then transfer the tin to the oven and bake for 15–20 minutes.

- Test with a wooden toothpick, if it comes out clean, the cakes are done. Transfer the cakes to a wire rack and leave to cool completely.

- Reserve a small amount of icing for the labels and dye the rest pink.

- Shape the pink icing into 12 bottle shapes.

- Roll out the white icing until very thin.

- Cut out 12 labels with a scalpel and attach them to the bottles with a dab of water.

- Roll the off-cuts into 12 small corks and attach each one to the top of a bottle with a dab of water.

- Beat the butter until smooth, then gradually whisk in the icing sugar and vanilla extract.

- Spoon the mixture into a piping bag, fitted with a large star nozzle and pipe 2 large rosettes of buttercream on top of each other on each cake.

- Press a champagne bottle into the top of each cake and dust with edible glitter.

Polka Dot Cupcakes

Ingredients

110 g / 4 oz / ⅔ cup self-raising flour, sifted

110 g / 4 oz / ½ cup caster (superfine) sugar

110 g / 4 oz / ½ cup butter, softened

2 large eggs

1 tsp vanilla extract

To Decorate

100 g / 3 ½ oz / ½ cup butter, softened

200 g / 7 oz / 2 cups icing (confectioners') sugar

½ tsp vanilla extract

100 g / 3 ½ oz / ¼ cup ready to roll fondant icing

pink and purple food dye

12

Makes

75

Preparation Time (Minutes)

15–20

Cooking Time (Minutes)

Methods

- Preheat the oven to 190°C (170°C fan) / 375F / gas 5 and line a 12-hole cupcake tin with paper cases.

- Combine the flour, sugar, butter, eggs and vanilla extract in a bowl and whisk together for 2 minutes or until smooth. Divide the mixture between the cases, then transfer the tin to the oven and bake for 15–20 minutes.

- Test with a wooden toothpick, if it comes out clean, the cakes are done. Transfer the cakes to a wire rack and leave to cool completely.

- Beat the butter until smooth, then gradually whisk in the icing sugar and vanilla extract.

- Spoon the buttercream into a piping bag, fitted with a large star nozzle and pipe a big swirl on top of each cake.

- Dye half of the fondant icing pink and the other half purple.

- Roll out the icing and use a 1.5 cm (½ in) plunger cutter to cut circles out of the pink and purple icing.

- Transfer the polka dots to the cakes and press them lightly into the buttercream.

Green Ribbon Cupcakes

Ingredients

110 g / 4 oz / ⅔ cup self-raising
  flour, sifted

110 g / 4 oz / ½ cup caster
  (superfine) sugar

110 g / 4 oz / ½ cup butter, softened

2 large eggs

2 tbsp unsweetened cocoa powder

To Decorate

100 g / 3 ½ oz ready to roll
  fondant icing

green food dye

100 g / 3 ½ oz / ½ cup butter,
  softened

200 g / 7 oz / 2 cups icing
  (confectioners') sugar

½ tsp vanilla extract

green sugar sprinkles

12

Makes

120

Preparation Time
(Minutes)

15–20

Cooking Time
(Minutes)

overnight

Setting Time

Methods

- Preheat the oven to 190°C (170°C fan) / 375F / gas 5 and line a 12-hole cupcake tin with paper cases.

- Combine the flour, sugar, butter, eggs and cocoa powder in a bowl and whisk together for 2 minutes or until smooth. Divide the mixture between the cases, then transfer the tin to the oven and bake for 15–20 minutes.

- Test with a wooden toothpick, if it comes out clean, the cakes are done. Transfer the cakes to a wire rack and leave to cool completely.

- Dye the fondant icing pale green, kneading until all the streaks of dye have disappeared.

- Dust the work surface lightly with icing sugar and roll out the icing.

- Cut the icing into long strips with a multi-cutter.

- Wrap each strip of icing in a spiral around a wooden dowel and leave to set and harden overnight.

- Beat the butter until smooth, then gradually whisk in the icing sugar and vanilla extract.

- Dye the buttercream pale green and spread half of it over the surface of the cakes.

- Spoon the rest of the buttercream into a piping bag, fitted with a plain nozzle and pipe a ring of teardrops round the edge of each cake.

- Sprinkle the centres with green sugar sprinkles.

- When the icing ribbons have hardened, carefully slide them off the dowels and arrange on top of the cakes.

Shooting Star Cupcakes

Ingredients

110 g / 4 oz / ⅔ cup self-raising
  flour, sifted
110 g / 4 oz / ½ cup caster
  (superfine) sugar
110 g / 4 oz / ½ cup butter, softened
2 large eggs
1 tsp vanilla extract

To Decorate

100 g / 3 ½ oz / ½ cup butter, softened
200 g / 7 oz / 2 cups icing
  (confectioners') sugar
½ tsp vanilla extract
200 g / 7 oz ready to roll fondant icing
pink food dye
48 floral wires

12

Makes

90

Preparation Time
(Minutes)

15–20

Cooking Time
(Minutes)

Methods

- Preheat the oven to 190°C (170°C fan) / 375F / gas 5 and line a 12-hole cupcake tin with paper cases.

- Combine the flour, sugar, butter, eggs and vanilla extract in a bowl and whisk together for 2 minutes or until smooth. Divide the mixture between the cases, then transfer the tin to the oven and bake for 15–20 minutes.

- Test with a wooden toothpick, if it comes out clean, the cakes are done. Transfer the cakes to a wire rack and leave to cool completely.

- Beat the butter until smooth, then gradually whisk in the icing sugar and vanilla extract.

- Spread the buttercream on top of the cakes and smooth the surface with a palette knife.

- Reserve a third of the fondant icing for the stars and dye the rest pink.

- Roll out the pink icing on a work surface and cut out 12 circles the same diameter as the top of the cupcakes with a fluted cookie cutter.

- Roll out the white icing.

- Cut out 60 medium sized stars and stick one star in the centre of each cake, securing with a dab of water.

- Use a small star plunger cutter to cut out 12 tiny stars for each cake and attach them round the outside of the cupcakes as before.

- Thread each remaining medium sized star onto a piece of floral wire.

- Insert 4 wires into each cake through the star in the centre and fan them out.

Presents Cupcakes

Ingredients

110 g / 4 oz / ⅔ cup self-raising
  flour, sifted
110 g / 4 oz / ½ cup caster
  (superfine) sugar
110 g / 4 oz / ½ cup butter, softened
2 large eggs
1 tsp vanilla extract

To Decorate

100 g / 3 ½ oz / ½ cup butter, softened
200 g / 7 oz / 2 cups icing
  (confectioners') sugar
½ tsp vanilla extract
300 g / 9 oz ready to roll fondant icing
pink food dye

12

Makes

75

Preparation Time
(Minutes)

15–20

Cooking Time
(Minutes)

Methods

- Preheat the oven to 190°C (170°C fan) / 375F / gas 5 and line a 12-hole cupcake tin with paper cases.

- Combine the flour, sugar, butter, eggs and vanilla extract in a bowl and whisk together for 2 minutes or until smooth. Divide the mixture between the cases, then transfer the tin to the oven and bake for 15–20 minutes.

- Test with a wooden toothpick, if it comes out clean, the cakes are done. Transfer the cakes to a wire rack and leave to cool completely.

- Beat the butter until smooth, then gradually whisk in the icing sugar and vanilla extract.

- Spoon the buttercream into a piping bag, fitted with a large star nozzle and pipe a big swirl on top of each cake.

- Reserve a small amount of icing to make the ribbons and dye the rest pink.

- Roll the pink icing into 12 balls with your hands.

- Cut the sides off of the balls to make them into cubes.

- Smooth the edges and sharpen the edges with your hands.

- Roll out the reserved white icing and cut it into thin ribbons with a pizza wheel.

- Paint a cross on top of each cube with a little water.

- Lay 2 white fondant ribbons across each box and smooth them down the sides. Trim off the ends with a scalpel.

- Make 12 tiny bows from the remaining white fondant ribbons.

- Attach the bows to the top of the presents with a dab of water.

- Roll some of the pink icing off-cuts into 12 tiny balls and use as the centres of the bows.

- Position a present on top of each cupcake.

Special Occasions

Candles Cupcakes

Ingredients

110 g / 4 oz / ⅔ cup self-raising flour, sifted

110 g / 4 oz / ½ cup caster (superfine) sugar

110 g / 4 oz / ½ cup butter, softened

2 large eggs

1 tsp vanilla extract

To Decorate

100 g / 3 ½ oz / ½ cup butter, softened

200 g / 7 oz / 2 cups icing (confectioners') sugar

½ tsp vanilla extract

edible pink glitter

96 birthday candles

96 candle holders

12

Makes

60

Preparation Time (Minutes)

15–20

Cooking Time (Minutes)

Methods

- Preheat the oven to 190°C (170°C fan) / 375F / gas 5 and line a 12-hole cupcake tin with paper cases.

- Combine the flour, sugar, butter, eggs and vanilla extract in a bowl and whisk together for 2 minutes or until smooth. Divide the mixture between the cases, then transfer the tin to the oven and bake for 15–20 minutes.

- Test with a wooden toothpick, if it comes out clean, the cakes are done. Transfer the cakes to a wire rack and leave to cool completely.

- Beat the butter until smooth, then gradually whisk in the icing sugar and vanilla extract.

- Spoon the icing into a piping bag fitted with a large star nozzle.

- Pipe 8 rosettes of icing on top of each cake.

- Use a dry paint brush to sprinkle a little pink edible glitter over the top of each cake.

- Insert each candle into a candle holder.

- Stick a candle in the top of each icing rosette and light them just before serving.

Birthday Number Cupcakes

Ingredients

110 g / 4 oz / ⅔ cup self-raising flour, sifted

110 g / 4 oz / ½ cup caster (superfine) sugar

110 g / 4 oz / ½ cup butter, softened

2 large eggs

1 lemon, juiced and zest finely grated

To Decorate

400 g / 14 oz / 1 cup ready to roll fondant icing

blue food dye

icing (confectioners') sugar for dusting

edible ink pens

Makes

Preparation Time (Minutes)

Cooking Time (Minutes)

Methods

- Preheat the oven to 190°C (170°C fan) / 375F / gas 5 and line a 12-hole cupcake tin with paper cases.

- Combine the flour, sugar, butter, eggs and lemon juice and zest in a bowl and whisk together for 2 minutes or until smooth. Divide the mixture between the cases, then transfer the tin to the oven and bake for 15–20 minutes.

- Test with a wooden toothpick, if it comes out clean, the cakes are done. Transfer the cakes to a wire rack and leave to cool completely.

- Dye half of the fondant icing blue. Dust the work surface lightly with icing sugar and roll out the blue icing. Use a cookie cutter the same diameter as the top of the cakes to cut out 12 circles then attach them

to the top of the cakes with a dab of water.

- Roll out the white fondant icing until 2 mm thick.

- Use a large flower-shaped cutter to cut out 12 flowers.

- Attach a flower to the top of each cake, securing with a dab of water.

- Briefly knead the blue icing off-cuts and roll them out until 4 mm thick.

- Use a number-shaped cutter to cut out 12 numbers.

- Brush the back of each number with a little water, then attach one to the centre of each flower.

Butterfly Cupcakes

Ingredients

110 g / 4 oz / ⅔ cup self-raising flour, sifted

110 g / 4 oz / ½ cup caster (superfine) sugar

110 g / 4 oz / ½ cup butter, softened

2 large eggs

2 tbsp unsweetened cocoa powder

To Decorate

110 g / 4 oz ready to roll fondant icing

orange food dye powder

100 g / 3 ½ oz / ½ cup butter, softened

200 g / 7 oz / 2 cups icing (confectioners') sugar

½ tsp vanilla extract

12

Makes

70

Preparation Time (Minutes)

15–20

Cooking Time (Minutes)

overnight

Setting Time

Methods

- Preheat the oven to 190°C (170°C fan) / 375F / gas 5 and line a 12-hole cupcake tin with paper cases.

- Combine the flour, sugar, butter, eggs and cocoa powder in a bowl and whisk together for 2 minutes or until smooth. Divide the mixture between the cases, then transfer the tin to the oven and bake for 15–20 minutes.

- Test with a wooden toothpick, if it comes out clean, the cakes are done. Transfer the cakes to a wire rack and leave to cool completely.

- Roll out the fondant icing and cut out 12 butterfly shapes.

- Fold a piece of card in half to make a 'v' shape and lay the butterflies down the centre. Leave to set and harden overnight.

- Put a little orange food dye powder in a plastic tray and add a few drops of water to make a paint.

- Paint the edge of the wings and the body onto the butterflies then add a spot to each wing.

- Beat the butter until smooth, then gradually whisk in the icing sugar, vanilla extract and a little of the orange food dye powder.

- Spoon the mixture into a piping bag, fitted with a large star nozzle. Starting in the centre, pipe the icing on in a spiral, keeping the piping bag completely vertical to produce a rose effect.

- Press a butterfly onto the side of each one.

Vanilla Sprinkles Cakes

Ingredients

125 g / 4 ½ oz / ½ cup butter
  unsalted, softened

125 g / 4 ½ oz / ½ cup caster
  (superfine) sugar

2 medium eggs, room temperature

½ tsp vanilla extract

125 g / 4 ½ oz / 1 cup self-raising
  flour

45 ml / 1 ½ fl. oz / ¼ cup milk

To Decorate

125 g / 4 ½ oz / ½ cup butter,
  unsalted, softened

300 g / 10 ½ oz / 2 ½ cups icing
  (confectioners') sugar

½ tsp vanilla extract

½ tbsp. milk

Sprinkles

12

Makes

20

Preparation Time
(Minutes)

18–20

Cooking Time
(Minutes)

Methods

- Preheat the oven to 180°C (160°C fan) / 350F / gas 4 and line a cupcake tin with paper cases.

- Cream the butter and sugar until pale and fluffy with an electric whisk.

- Gradually mix in the eggs and vanilla extract.

- Gently mix in the flour whilst adding the milk.

- Spoon some cupcake mix into each paper case.

- Bake, for 18–20 minutes. Test with a wooden toothpick, if it comes out clean, the cake are done.

- Place on a wire rack to cool.

- To make the buttercream beat the butter with a whisk until soft and gradually beat in the icing sugar, vanilla and milk.

- Pipe buttercream and scatter sugar sprinkles on top.

Glitter Magic Cupcakes

Ingredients

225 g / 8 oz / 1 cup butter, softened

250 g / 9 oz / 1 ¼ cups caster (superfine) sugar

3 eggs

1 tsp vanilla extract

300 g / 11 oz / 2 ½ cups plain (all purpose) flour

1 ½ tsp baking powder

¼ tsp baking soda

¼ tsp salt
240 ml / 8 ½ fl. oz / 1 cup buttermilk

To Decorate

125 g / 4 ½ oz / ½ cup butter, unsalted, softened

300 g / 10 ½ oz / 2 ½ cups icing (confectioners') sugar

½ tsp vanilla extract

½ tbsp. milk

edible glitter

pink pearls

Makes

Preparation Time (Minutes)

Cooking Time (Minutes)

Methods

- Preheat the oven to 180°C (160° fan) / 350F / gas 4 and line a cupcake tin with paper cases.

- Cream the butter and sugar until light and fluffy.

- Gradually beat in the eggs and vanilla.

- Combine the flour, baking powder, baking soda and salt; add to the creamed mixture alternately with buttermilk, beating well after each addition.

- Spoon some cupcake mix into each paper case.

- Bake, for 18–20 minutes. Test with a wooden toothpick, if it comes out clean, the cake are done.

- Place on a wire rack to cool.

- To make the buttercream beat the butter with a whisk until soft, and gradually beat in the icing sugar, vanilla and milk.

- Pipe buttercream swirls onto the cupcakes. Sprinkle with edible glitter and place pink pearls on top.

Birthday Blues Cupcakes

Ingredients

115 g / 4 oz / ½ cup butter, unsalted, softened

115 g / 4 oz / ½ cup caster (superfine) sugar

2 large eggs

1 tsp vanilla extract

115 g / 4 0z / 1 cup plain (all purpose) flour

1 tsp baking powder

2–3 tbsp milk

2–3 tsp cinnamon

75 g / 3 oz / ½ demerara sugar

To Decorate

125 g / 4 ½ oz / ½ cup butter, unsalted, softened

300 g / 10 ½ oz / 2 ½ cups icing (confectioners') sugar

½ tsp vanilla extract

½ tbsp. milk

edible glitter

candle

Makes

Preparation Time (Minutes)

Cooking Time (Minutes)

Methods

- Preheat the oven to 180°C (160°C fan) / 350F / gas 4 and line a cupcake tin with paper cases.

- Cream the butter and sugar until pale and fluffy with an electric whisk.

- Gradually mix in the eggs and vanilla extract.

- Gently mix in the flour and baking powder whilst adding the milk.

- In a separate bowl mix together demerara sugar and cinnamon.

- Pour a small amount of the cupcake mix into the cases, enough to cover bottom of the case. Add 1 tsp of cinnamon sugar. Repeat and top with a layer of cupcake mixture.

- Take a toothpick and poke into the centre of each cupcake case. Swirl around to stir up mix and cinnamon sugar.

- Bake, for 20 minutes. Test with a wooden toothpick, if it comes out clean, the cakes are done.

- Place on a wire rack to cool.

- To make the buttercream beat the butter with a whisk until soft, and gradually beat in the icing sugar, vanilla and milk.

- Pipe buttercream swirls onto each cake. Sprinkle with edible glitter and insert a candle.

Strawberry Surprise Cupcakes

Ingredients

8 large fresh strawberries or as needed

2 eggs

200 g / 7 oz / 1 cup caster (superfine) sugar

75 ml / 2 ½ oz / ¼ cup vegetable oil

½ tsp vanilla extract

½ tsp grated lemon zest

200 g / 7 oz / 1 ½ cup plain (all purpose) flour

2 tsp baking powder

¼ tsp salt

3 tbsp custard powder (optional)

To Decorate

175 g / 6 oz / ¾ cup cream cheese, softened

30 g / 1 oz / ¼ cup butter, unsalted, softened

60 g / 2 oz / ½ cup icing (confectioners') sugar

½ tsp vanilla extract

15

Makes

40

Preparation Time (Minutes)

20

Cooking Time (Minutes)

Methods

- Preheat the oven to 170°C (150°C fan) / 325F / gas 3 and line a cupcake tin with paper cases.

- Blend the strawberries until smooth. Poor the puree through a sieve to remove any seeds.

- Beat together the eggs, sugar, oil, vanilla extract, lemon zest and strawberry puree until well combined.

- Stir in the flour, baking powder, salt and custard powder.

- Spoon some cupcake mix into each paper case.

- Bake, for 20 minutes. Test with a wooden toothpick, if it comes out clean, the cakes are done.

- Place on a wire rack to cool.

- To make the cream cheese icing beat the butter and cream cheese together until smooth and gradually mix in the icing sugar and vanilla.

- Pipe icing.

J Heart Chocolate

Ingredients

75 g / 3 oz / ½ cup dark chocolate, broken

200 g / 7 oz / 1 cup butter, unsalted, softened

225 g / 8 oz / 1 cup caster (superfine) sugar

3 eggs

½ tsp baking powder

175 g / 6 oz / 1 ½ cups plain (all purpose) flour

25 g / 1 oz / ¼ cup cocoa powder

50 g / 2 oz / ½ cup dark chocolate chips

To Decorate

175 g / 6 oz / ¾ cup cream cheese, softened

30 g / 1 oz / ¼ cup butter, unsalted, softened

60 g / 2 oz / ½ cup icing (confectioners') sugar

½ tsp vanilla extract

chocolate hearts

12

Makes

20

Preparation Time (Minutes)

20–25

Cooking Time (Minutes)

Methods

- Preheat the oven to 200°C (180°C fan) / 400 F / gas 6 and line a cupcake tin with paper cases.

- In a large saucepan, melt the chocolate and butter over medium heat, stirring to prevent burning. Allow this to cool for a few minutes

- Stir in the sugar until well mixed. Add the eggs, one at a time, until you have a smooth batter. Sift the baking powder, flour and cocoa into the batter and mix until smooth. Fold in the chocolate chips.

- Spoon some cupcake mix into each paper case.

- Bake, for 20–25 minutes. Test with a wooden toothpick, if it comes out clean, the cakes are done.

- Place on a wire rack to cool.

- To make the cream cheese icing beat the butter and cream cheese together until smooth and gradually mix in the icing sugar and vanilla.

- Pipe icing swirls and add a chocolate heart onto each cake.

Gluten-free Butterfly Cupcakes

Ingredients

150 g / 5 ½ oz / ½ cup butter, unsalted, softened

150 g/ 5 ½ oz / ½ cup golden caster (superfine) sugar

150 g / 5 ½ oz / 1 cup gluten-free self-raising flour

3 eggs

To Decorate

125 g / 4 ½ oz / ½ cup butter, unsalted, softened

300 g / 10 ½ oz / 2 ½ cups icing (confectioners') sugar

½ tsp vanilla extract

½ tbsp. milk

fondant butterflies

12

Makes

15

Preparation Time
(Minutes)

20

Cooking Time
(Minutes)

Methods

- Preheat the oven to 180°C (160° fan) / 350F / gas 4 and line a cupcake tin with paper cases.

- Cream the butter and sugar until pale and fluffy with an electric whisk.

- Gradually mix in the eggs.

- Gently mix in the flour.

- Spoon some cupcake mix into each paper case.

- Bake, for 20 minutes. Test with a wooden toothpick, if it comes out clean, the cakes are done.

- Place on a wire rack to cool.

- To make the buttercream beat the butter with a whisk until soft, and gradually beat in the icing sugar, vanilla and milk.

- Pipe buttercream swirls and add a butterfly to each cupcake.

Sammy Snake Cupcakes

Ingredients

150 g / 5 ½ oz / ½ cup margarine

150 g / 5 ½ oz / ½ cup caster (superfine) sugar

100 g / 3 ½ oz / ¾ cup self-raising flour

3 eggs, at room temperature

1 tsp baking powder

60 g / 2 ¼ oz / ½ cup ground almonds

1 tbsp milk

To Decorate

125 g / 4 ½ oz / ½ cup butter, unsalted, softened

300 g / 10 ½ oz / 2 ½ cups icing (confectioners') sugar

½ tsp vanilla extract

½ tbsp. milk

12

Makes

30

Preparation Time (Minutes)

20

Cooking Time (Minutes)

Methods

- Preheat the oven to 180°C (160°C fan) / 350F / gas 4 and line a cupcake tin with paper cases.

- Cream the margarine and sugar until pale and fluffy with an electric whisk.

- Gradually mix in the egg and vanilla extract.

- Gently mix in the flour, ground almonds and baking powder, adding the milk.

- Spoon some cupcake mix into each paper case.

- Bake, for 20 minutes. Test with a wooden toothpick, if it comes out clean, the cakes are done.

- Place on a wire rack to cool.

- To make the buttercream beat the butter with a whisk until soft, and gradually beat in the icing sugar, vanilla and milk.

- Pipe buttercream in a spiral onto each cupcake. Add pearls for the snakes eyes.

Strawberry Ripple Cupcakes

Ingredients

150g / 5 ½ oz / ½ cup butter, room temperature

150g / 5 ½ oz / ½ cup caster (superfine) sugar

3 eggs, at room temperature

150g / 5 ½ oz / ½ cup self-raising flour

1 tsp baking powder

¼ tsp salt

4 tbsp finely chopped fresh strawberries, drained

To Decorate

125 g / 4 ½ oz / ½ cup butter, unsalted, softened

300 g / 10 ½ oz / 2 ½ cups icing (confectioners') sugar

½ tsp vanilla extract

½ tbsp. milk

4 tbsp finely chopped fresh strawberries, drained

Fondant flowers

12

Makes

15

Preparation Time (Minutes)

20

Cooking Time (Minutes)

Methods

• Preheat the oven to 170°C (150°C fan) / 325F / gas 3 and line a cupcake tin with paper cases.

• Cream the butter and sugar until pale and fluffy with an electric whisk.

• Gradually mix in the eggs.

• Gently mix in the flour and salt.

• Fold in the strawberries.

• Spoon some cupcake mix into each paper case.

• Bake, for 20 minutes. Test with a wooden toothpick, if it comes out clean, the cakes are done.

• Place on a wire rack to cool.

• To make the buttercream beat the butter with a whisk until soft, and gradually beat in the icing sugar, vanilla, strawberries and milk.

• Pipe buttercream onto each cake.

• Top with a fondant flower.

Strawberry Jam-filled Cupcakes

Ingredients

125 g / 4 ½ oz / ½ cup butter
 unsalted, softened

125 g / 4 ½ oz / ½ cup caster
 (superfine) sugar

2 medium eggs, room temperature

½ tsp vanilla extract

125 g / 4 ½ oz / 1 cup self-raising flour

45 ml / 1 ½ fl. oz / ¼ cup milk

To Decorate

125 g / 4 ½ oz / ½ cup butter

300 g / 10 ½ oz / 2 ½ cups icing
 (confectioners') sugar

½ tsp vanilla extract

½ tbsp. milk

150 g / 5 ½ oz / 1 cup strawberry jam
 (jelly)

12

Makes

20

Preparation Time
(Minutes)

18–20

Cooking Time
(Minutes)

Methods

- Preheat the oven to 180°C (160°C fan) / 350F / gas 4 and line a cupcake tin with paper cases.

- Cream the butter and sugar until pale and fluffy with an electric whisk.

- Gradually mix in the eggs and vanilla extract.

- Gently mix in the flour adding the milk.

- Spoon cupcake mix into each paper case.

- Bake, for 18–20 minutes. Test with a wooden toothpick, if it comes out clean, the cakes are done.

- Place on a wire rack to cool.

- Scoop a small hole out of each cupcake and fill with 1 tsp jam.

- To make the buttercream beat the butter with a whisk until soft, and gradually beat in the icing sugar, vanilla and milk.

- Pipe buttercream and spoon a little more jam into the centre of each cupcake.

Pink Butterfly Cupcakes

Ingredients

125 g / 4 ½ oz / ½ cup butter
  unsalted, softened
125 g / 4 ½ oz / ½ cup caster
  (superfine) sugar
2 medium eggs, room temperature
½ tsp vanilla extract
125 g / 4 ½ oz / 1 cup self-raising
  flour
45 ml / 1 ½ fl. oz / ¼ cup milk
10 strawberries

To Decorate

125 g / 4 ½ oz / ½ cup butter
300 g / 10 ½ oz / 2 ½ cups icing
  (confectioners') sugar
1 tsp strawberry essence
½ tbsp milk

10

Makes

20

Preparation Time
(Minutes)

18–20

Cooking Time
(Minutes)

Methods

- Preheat the oven to 180°C (160°C fan) / 350F / gas 4 and line a cupcake tin with paper cases.

- Cream the butter and sugar until pale and fluffy with an electric whisk.

- Gradually mix in the eggs and vanilla extract.

- Gently mix in the flour adding the milk.

- Spoon some cupcake mix into each paper case.

- Bake, for 18–20 minutes. Test with a wooden toothpick, if it comes out clean, the cakes are done.

- Place on a wire rack to cool.

- Cut and remove a strawberry (coned) shaped portion of cupcake from the top of each cupcake, leaving about 2cm of cake in the bottom. Stuff each cupcake with a strawberry and cover with a little bit of the removed cake.

- To make the buttercream beat the butter with a whisk until soft, and gradually beat in the icing sugar, vanilla and milk.

- Pipe buttercream swirls onto each cake. Place a butterfly on top.

Coming Up Roses Cupcakes

Ingredients

3 Earl Grey tea bags

120 ml / 4 ½ oz / ½ cup whole milk

140 g / 5 oz / ½ cup caster
(superfine) sugar

1 ½ tsp baking powder

pinch of salt

40 g / 2 oz / ¼ cup butter, unsalted,
softened

1 egg

To Decorate

125 g / 4 ½ oz / ½ cup butter

300 g / 10 ½ oz / 2 ½ cups icing sugar

½ tsp vanilla extract

½ tbsp. milk

fondant rose

Makes

**Preparation Time
(Minutes)**

**Cooking Time
(Minutes)**

Methods

- Place the teabags and milk in a saucepan and gently heat to brew the tea, leave to cool, overnight if possible.

- Preheat the oven to 190°C (170°C fan) / 375F / gas 5 and line a cupcake tin with paper cases.

- Mix the butter, sugar, flour, baking powder and salt on a low speed until it is the texture of breadcrumbs.

- Put the eggs in a jug and whisk by hand.

- Add the tea infused milk to the eggs.

- Pour ¾ of the milk mixture into the dry ingredients and mix on low speed, then mix on a medium speed until smooth and thick.

- Spoon some cupcake mix into each paper case.

- Bake, for 18–20 minutes. Test with a wooden toothpick, if it comes out clean, the cakes are done.

- Place on a wire rack to cool.

- To make the buttercream beat the butter with a whisk until soft, and gradually beat in the icing sugar, vanilla and milk.

- Pipe buttercream swirls onto each cake. Place a fondant rose on top.

Candy Hearts Cupcakes

Ingredients

2 eggs

175 g / 6 oz / 1 cup brown muscovado sugar

150 ml / 5 ½ fl. oz / ½ cup sunflower oil

100 g / 3 ½ oz / 1 cup wholemeal self-raising flour

100 g / 3 ½ oz / 1 cup self-raising flour

½ tsp ground ginger

½ tsp ground cloves or nutmeg

1 tsp cinnamon

1 tsp bicarbonate of baking soda

1 tsp vanilla extract

200 g / 7 oz / 1 ½ cups carrots, grated

2 oranges, zested

To Decorate

450 g / 16 oz / 3 ½ cups icing sugar

75 g / 2 ½ oz / ⅓ cup butter, unsalted, softened

185 g / 6 ½ oz / 1 cup cream cheese

candy hearts

Makes

Preparation Time (Minutes)

Cooking Time (Minutes)

Methods

- Preheat the oven to 180°C (160°C fan) / 350F / gas 4 and line cupcake tins with paper cases.

- Beat the eggs, sugar and oil in a large bowl for 3 minutes until light and fluffy.

- Gently fold in the flour, spices, bicarbonate of soda, vanilla extract, grated carrot, and half the orange zest, until thoroughly combined.

- Divide the mixture between the cases and bake for 20–25 minutes. Test with a wooden toothpick, if it comes out clean, the cakes are done. Leave to cool.

- Beat the icing sugar and butter together on a medium speed until well mixed.

- Add all of the cream cheese and beat for 5 minutes or until you have reached the desired consistency.

- Pipe buttercream pillows onto each cake. Place a candy heart on top of each cake.

Sweet Treats Cupcakes

Ingredients

110 g / 4 oz / ⅔ cup self-raising flour, sifted

110 g / 4 oz / ½ cup margarine, softened

110 g / 4 oz / ½ cup caster (superfine) sugar

1 tsp vanilla extract

2 large eggs

a pinch of salt

To Decorate

225 g / 8 oz / 1 cup unsalted butter, softened

180 g / 6 oz / 1 ½ cups icing (confectioners') sugar

1 tsp vanilla extract

100 g / 3 ½ oz / ½ cup assorted little sweets

12 white chocolate buttons

12 raspberry jelly sweets

12

Makes

10

Preparation Time (Minutes)

15–18

Cooking Time (Minutes)

Methods

- Preheat the oven to 180°C (160°C fan) / 350F / gas 4.

- Line a 12-hole cupcake tin with 12 cupcake cases.

- Beat together all the ingredients for the batter in a mixing bowl for 2 minutes until smooth and creamy.

- Divide evenly between the paper cases before rapping the tin on a work surface to help settle the batter.

- Bake for 15–18 minutes until risen; test with a wooden toothpick, if it comes out clean, the cakes are done.

- Remove to a wire rack to cool as you prepare the buttercream.

- Beat the softened butter for 2 minutes until creamy and pale.

- Add the icing sugar and vanilla extract and beat well until smooth.

- Spoon into a piping bag fitted with a star-shaped nozzle and pipe stars of buttercream on top of the cupcakes.

- Decorate with the assorted little sweets, white chocolate buttons and jelly sweets.

Irresistible Dark Chocolate Cupcakes

Ingredients

110 g / 4 oz / ⅔ cup self-raising flour, sifted

110 ml / 4 fl. oz / ½ cup sunflower oil

110 g / 4 oz / ½ cup caster (superfine) sugar

75 g / 3 oz / ½ cup cocoa powder

30 g / 1 oz / 2 tbsp cornflour (cornstarch)

1 tbsp distilled vinegar

2 large eggs

a pinch of salt

To Decorate

175 g / 6 oz / ¾ cup unsalted butter, softened

125 g / 4 ½ oz / 1 cup icing (confectioners') sugar

50 g / 2 oz / ⅓ cup cocoa powder

2 tbsp whole milk

55 g / 2 oz / ¼ cup sprinkles

12

Makes

15

Preparation Time (Minutes)

15–18

Cooking Time (Minutes)

Methods

- Preheat the oven to 180°C (160°C fan) / 350F / gas 4.

- Line a 12-hole cupcake tin with 12 cupcake cases.

- Beat together all the ingredients for the batter in a mixing bowl for 2 minutes until smooth.

- Divide evenly between the paper cases before rapping the tin on a work surface to help settle the batter.

- Bake for 15–18 minutes until risen; test with a wooden toothpick, if it comes out clean, the cakes are done.

- Remove to a wire rack to cool as you prepare the buttercream.

- Beat the softened butter with the cocoa powder, icing sugar and milk in a mixing bowl until smooth and creamy.

- Spoon into a piping bag fitted with a straight-sided nozzle and pipe in mounds on top of the cupcakes.

- Decorate the buttercream with a few of the sprinkles before serving.

Chocolate Butterfly Cupcakes

Ingredients

110 g / 4 oz / ⅔ cup self-raising
flour, sifted

110 g / 4 oz / ½ cup margarine,
softened

110 g / 4 oz / ½ cup caster
(superfine) sugar

1 tsp vanilla extract

2 large eggs

a pinch of salt

To Decorate

175 g / 6 oz / ¾ cup unsalted butter,
softened

125 g / 4 ½ oz / 1 cup icing
(confectioners') sugar

50 g / 2 oz / ⅓ cup cocoa powder

2 tbsp whole milk

chocolate or fondant butterflies

12

Makes

10

Preparation Time
(Minutes)

Methods

- Preheat the oven to 180°C (160°C fan) / 350F / gas 4.

- Line a 12-hole cupcake tin with 12 cupcake cases.

- Beat together all the ingredients for the batter in a mixing bowl for 2 minutes until smooth and creamy.

- Divide evenly between the paper cases before rapping the tin on a work surface to help settle the batter.

- Bake for 15–18 minutes until risen; test with a wooden toothpick, if it comes out clean, the cakes are done.

- Remove to a wire rack to cool as you prepare the buttercream.

- Beat the softened butter with the cocoa powder, icing sugar and milk in a mixing bowl until smooth and creamy.

- Spoon into a piping bag fitted with a straight-sided nozzle and pipe in round mounds on top of the cupcakes.

- Decorate the buttercream with a chocolate butterfly before serving.

15–18

Cooking Time
(Minutes)

Choco-Latte Cupcakes

Ingredients

110 g / 4 oz / ⅔ cup self-raising flour, sifted

110 g / 4 oz / ½ cup margarine, softened

110 g / 4 oz / ½ cup caster (superfine) sugar

1 tsp vanilla extract

2 large eggs

a pinch of salt

To Decorate

110 g / 4 oz / ½ cup unsalted butter, softened

65 g / 2 ½ oz / ½ cup icing (confectioners') sugar

2 tbsp cocoa powder

1 tbsp whole milk

100 g / 3 ½ oz / ⅔ cup milk chocolate, chopped

1 tsp coffee granules

12

Makes

10

Preparation Time (Minutes)

15–18

Cooking Time (Minutes)

Methods

- Preheat the oven to 180°C (160°C fan) / 350F / gas 4.

- Line a 12-hole cupcake tin with 12 cupcake cases.

- Beat together all the ingredients for the batter in a mixing bowl for 2 minutes until smooth and creamy.

- Divide evenly between the paper cases before rapping the tin on a work surface to help settle the batter.

- Bake for 15–18 minutes until risen; test with a wooden toothpick, if it comes out clean, the cakes are done.

- Remove to a wire rack to cool as you prepare the buttercream.

- Beat the softened butter with the cocoa powder, icing sugar and milk in a mixing bowl until smooth and creamy.

- Spoon into a piping bag fitted with a straight-sided nozzle and pipe in round blobs on top of the cupcakes.

- Melt the chopped chocolate in a heatproof bowl set atop a saucepan of simmering water, stirring occasionally.

- Remove from the heat and drizzle in pretzel-like shapes onto a greaseproof-lined baking tray.

- Let the shapes chill for 15 minutes before removing and peeling away from the greaseproof paper.

- Decorate the cupcakes with the chocolate shapes and a sprinkle of coffee granules before serving.

Coffee Truffle Cupcakes

Ingredients

110 g / 4 oz / ⅔ cup self-raising flour, sifted

110 g / 4 oz / ½ cup margarine, softened

110 g / 4 oz / ½ cup caster (superfine) sugar

55 g / 2 oz / ⅓ cup cocoa powder

55 ml / 2 fl. oz / ¼ cup whole milk

2 large eggs

a pinch of salt

To Decorate

175 g / 6 oz / ¾ cup unsalted butter, softened

125 g / 4 ½ oz / 1 cup icing (confectioners') sugar

50 g / 2 oz / ⅓ cup cocoa powder

2 tbsp whole milk

1 tbsp boiling water

1 tsp strong instant espresso powder

1 tsp pink dragée balls

1 tsp white dragée balls

12

Makes

10

Preparation Time (Minutes)

15–18

Cooking Time (Minutes)

Methods

- Preheat the oven to 180°C (160°C fan) / 350F / gas 4.

- Line a 12-hole cupcake tin with 12 cupcake cases.

- Beat together all the ingredients for the batter apart from the milk in a mixing bowl for 2 minutes until smooth and creamy.

- Add the milk and beat again for a further minute.

- Divide evenly between the paper cases before rapping the tin on a work surface to help settle the batter.

- Bake for 15–18 minutes until risen; test with a wooden toothpick, if it comes out clean, the cakes are done.

- Remove to a wire rack to cool as you prepare the buttercream.

- Beat the softened butter with the cocoa powder, icing sugar and milk in a mixing bowl until smooth and creamy.

- Mix together the espresso powder with the boiling water until smooth, then beat into the buttercream.

- Spoon into a piping bag fitted with a star-shaped nozzle and pipe a swirled mound on top of each cupcake.

- Decorate the buttercream with a few dragée balls before serving.

Raspberry Jelly Sweet Cupcakes

Ingredients

110 g / 4 oz / ⅔ cup self-raising
  flour, sifted

110 g / 4 oz / ½ cup margarine,
  softened

110 g / 4 oz / ½ cup caster
  (superfine) sugar

1 tsp vanilla extract

2 large eggs

a pinch of salt

To Decorate

225 g / 8 oz / 1 cup unsalted butter,
  softened

180 g / 6 oz / 1 cup icing
  (confectioners') sugar

a few drops of red food dye

12 raspberry jelly sweets

12

Makes

10

Preparation Time
(Minutes)

15–18

Cooking Time
(Minutes)

Methods

- Preheat the oven to 180°C (160°C fan) / 350F / gas 4.

- Line a 12-hole cupcake tin with 12 cupcake cases.

- Beat together all the ingredients for the batter in a mixing bowl for 2 minutes until smooth and creamy.

- Divide evenly between the paper cases before rapping the tin on a work surface to help settle the batter.

- Bake for 15–18 minutes until risen; test with a wooden toothpick, if it comes out clean, the cakes are done.

- Remove to a wire rack to cool as you prepare the buttercream.

- Beat the softened butter in a mixing bowl for 3–4 minutes until pale.

- Add the icing sugar and beat well before beating in the food dye until you reach a light pink dye.

- Spread evenly on top of the cupcakes using a small palette knife, reserving about a third of the icing.

- Spoon the remaining icing into a piping bag fitted with a star-shaped nozzle.

- Pipe a blob of icing on top of the level icing and decorate with a jelly sweet.

Lavender Buttercream Cupcakes

Ingredients

110 g / 4 oz / ⅔ cup self-raising flour, sifted

110 g / 4 oz / ½ cup margarine, softened

110 g / 4 oz / ½ cup caster (superfine) sugar

1 tsp vanilla extract

2 large eggs

a pinch of salt

To Decorate

225 g / 8 oz / 1 cup unsalted butter, softened

180 g / 6 oz / 1 ½ cups icing (confectioner's) sugar

a few drops of purple food dye

5 drops of lavender essence

12 raspberry Jelly Tots

12

Makes

10

Preparation Time (Minutes)

20

Cooking Time (Minutes)

Methods

- Preheat the oven to 180°C (160° fan) / 350F / gas 4.

- Line a 12-hole cupcake tin with 12 cupcake cases.

- Beat together all the ingredients for the batter in a mixing bowl for 2 minutes until smooth and creamy.

- Divide evenly between the paper cases before rapping the tin on a work surface to help settle the batter.

- Bake for 15-18 minutes until risen; test with a wooden toothpick, if it comes out clean, the cakes are done.

- Remove to a wire rack to cool as you prepare the buttercream.

- Beat the softened butter in a mixing bowl for 3-4 minutes until pale.

- Add the icing sugar, lavender essence and drops of food dye until you have an even, purple buttercream.

- Spoon into a piping bag fitted with a small star-shaped nozzle.

- Pipe a rosette swirl in the centre of the cupcakes and surround with piped stars before decorating with a jelly sweet on top.

Sour Cream Cupcakes

Ingredients

110 g / 4 oz / ⅔ cup self-raising flour, sifted

110 g / 4 oz / ½ cup margarine, softened

110 g / 4 oz / ½ cup caster (superfine) sugar

1 tsp vanilla extract

2 large eggs

a pinch of salt

To Decorate

175 g / 6 oz / ¾ cup cream cheese, cold

175 g / 6 oz / 1 ½ cups icing (confectioners') sugar

55 g / 2 oz / ¼ cup sour cream

1 tsp vanilla extract

a few drops of blue food dye

12

Makes

10

Preparation Time (Minutes)

15–18

Cooking Time (Minutes)

Methods

- Preheat the oven to 180°C (160°C fan) / 350F / gas 4.

- Line a 12-hole cupcake tin with 12 cupcake cases.

- Beat together all the ingredients for the batter in a mixing bowl for 2 minutes until smooth and creamy.

- Divide evenly between the paper cases before rapping the tin on a work surface to help settle the batter.

- Bake for 15–18 minutes until risen; test with a wooden toothpick, if it comes out clean, the cakes are done.

- Remove to a wire rack to cool as you prepare the icing.

- Beat the cream cheese and sour cream in a mixing bowl before adding the icing sugar and vanilla extract.

- Spoon most of the icing into a piping bag fitted with a star-shaped nozzle.

- Add drops of the food dye to the remaining icing, beating well until purple in dye.

- Spoon into a small piping bag fitted with a small straight-sided nozzle.

- Pipe the plain vanilla icing in a swirl on top of the cupcakes before dotting with beads and a small tip of purple icing.

Fruit and Cream Cupcakes

Ingredients

110 g / 4 oz / ⅔ cup self-raising flour, sifted

110 g / 4 oz / ½ cup margarine, softened

110 g / 4 oz / ½ cup caster (superfine) sugar

1 tsp vanilla extract

2 large eggs

a pinch of salt

To Decorate

225 g / 8 oz / 1 cup unsalted butter, softened

180 g / 6 oz / 1 ½ cups icing (confectioners') sugar

1 tsp vanilla extract

12 physalis

12 raspberries

12 blackcurrants

1 kiwi fruit, cut into 12 pieces

Makes

Preparation Time (Minutes)

Cooking Time (Minutes)

Methods

- Preheat the oven to 180°C (160°C fan) / 350F / gas 4.

- Line a 12-hole cupcake tin with 12 cupcake cases.

- Beat together all the ingredients for the batter in a mixing bowl for 2 minutes until smooth and creamy.

- Divide evenly between the paper cases before rapping the tin on a work surface to help settle the batter.

- Bake for 15–18 minutes until risen; test with a wooden toothpick, if it comes out clean, the cakes are done.

- Remove to a wire rack to cool as you prepare the vanilla buttercream.

- Beat the softened butter for 2–3 minutes until creamy and pale.

- Add the icing sugar and vanilla extract and beat again until smooth.

- Spoon into a piping bag fitted with a straight-sided nozzle before piping mounds on top of the cupcakes.

- Press the fruit decoration into the buttercream before serving.

Jelly Mint Cupcakes

Ingredients

110 g / 4 oz / ⅔ cup self-raising
flour, sifted

110 g / 4 oz / ½ cup margarine,
softened

110 g / 4 oz / ½ cup caster
(superfine) sugar

1 tsp vanilla extract

2 large eggs

a pinch of salt

To Decorate

225 g / 8 oz / 1 cup unsalted butter,
softened

180 g / 6 oz / 1 ½ cups icing
(confectioners') sugar

½ tsp peppermint extract

a few drops of red food dye

a few drops of green food dye

12 raspberry jelly sweets

12

Makes

10

Preparation Time
(Minutes)

15–18

Cooking Time
(Minutes)

Methods

- Preheat the oven to 180°C (160°C fan) / 350F / gas 4.

- Line a 12-hole cupcake tin with 12 cupcake cases.

- Beat together all the ingredients for the batter in a mixing bowl for 2 minutes until smooth and creamy.

- Divide evenly between the paper cases before rapping the tin on a work surface to help settle the batter.

- Bake for 15–18 minutes until risen; test with a wooden toothpick, if it comes out clean, the cakes are done.

- Remove to a wire rack to cool as you prepare the buttercream.

- Beat the softened butter for 2 minutes until creamy and pale.

- Add the icing sugar and beat again until smooth before dividing into two bowls.

- Add the peppermint extract and a few drops of green food dye into one bowl and add a few drops of red food dye to the other, beating until pink.

- Spread the pink buttercream evenly on top of the cupcakes and spoon the green into a piping bag fitted with a petal tip.

- Pipe ruffles in a mound on top of the pink icing before decorating with a jelly sweet.

Violet Lemon Jelly Bean Cupcakes

Ingredients

110 g / 4 oz / ⅔ cup self-raising flour, sifted

110 g / 4 oz / ½ cup margarine, softened

110 g / 4 oz / ½ cup caster (superfine) sugar

1 tsp lemon extract

2 large eggs

a pinch of salt

To Decorate

225 g / 8 oz / 1 cup unsalted butter, softened

180 g / 6 oz / 1 ½ cups icing (confectioners') sugar

1 tsp violet extract

a few drops of purple food dye

36 pink jelly beans

12

Makes

10

Preparation Time (Minutes)

15–18

Cooking Time (Minutes)

Methods

- Preheat the oven to 180°C (160°C fan) / 350F / gas 4.

- Line a 12-hole cupcake tin with 12 cupcake cases.

- Beat together all the ingredients for the batter in a mixing bowl for 2 minutes until smooth and creamy.

- Divide evenly between the paper cases before rapping the tin on a work surface to help settle the batter.

- Bake for 15–18 minutes until risen; test with a wooden toothpick, if it comes out clean, the cakes are done.

- Remove to a wire rack to cool as you prepare the buttercream.

- Beat the softened butter for 2–3 minutes until creamy and pale.

- Add the icing sugar and violet extract and beat again until smooth.

- Spoon ⅔ into a piping bag fitted with a straight-sided nozzle before adding a few drops of food dye to the remaining buttercream.

- Beat well until the buttercream is violet and spoon into a piping bag fitted with a small star-shaped nozzle.

- Pipe pillows of the plain vanilla buttercream on top of the cupcakes before piping violet buttercream stars around them.

- Decorate with 3 jelly beans on each cupcake.

Mint Truffle Cupcakes

Ingredients

110 g / 4 oz / ⅔ cup self-raising flour, sifted

110 g / 4 oz / ½ cup margarine, softened

110 g / 4 oz / ½ cup caster (superfine) sugar

1 tsp vanilla extract

2 large eggs

a pinch of salt

To Decorate

300 g / 10 ½ oz / 1 ⅓ cups unsalted butter, softened

250 g / 9 oz / 2 cups icing (confectioners') sugar

1 tbsp cocoa powder

1 tbsp boiling water

½ tsp peppermint extract

a few drops of green food dye

12 hard shell chocolate sweets

1 tbsp sprinkles

12

Makes

10

Preparation Time
(Minutes)

15–18

Cooking Time
(Minutes)

Methods

- Preheat the oven to 180°C (160°C fan) / 350F / gas 4.

- Line a 12-hole cupcake tin with 12 cupcake cases.

- Beat together all the ingredients for the batter in a mixing bowl for 2 minutes until smooth and creamy.

- Divide evenly between the paper cases before rapping the tin on a work surface to help settle the batter.

- Bake for 15–18 minutes until risen; test with a wooden toothpick, if it comes out clean, the cakes are done.

- Remove to a wire rack to cool as you prepare the buttercream.

- Beat the softened butter and icing sugar for 2–3 minutes until creamy and pale.

- Divide between two bowls, adding the food dye and peppermint extract to one and the cocoa powder and boiling water to the other.

- Beat both well before spooning into separate piping bags fitted with star-shaped nozzles.

- Level the top of the cupcakes before piping spiral swirls of the chocolate buttercream on top followed with a spiral swirl of mint buttercream on top.

- Decorate with a hard shell chocolate sweet and a few of the sprinkles.

Index

ALMONDS, GROUND
Banoffee Pie Cupcakes, 81
Chocolate Cigarillo Cupcakes, 73
Raspberry Mess Cupcakes, 62
Sammy Snake Cupcakes, 185

AMARETTO LIQUEUR
Banoffee Pie Cupcakes, 81

APPLE PUREE
Summer Fruits Cupcakes, 24

BAILEYS LIQUEUR
Funky Toadstool Cupcakes, 122

BANANA
Banoffee Pie Cupcakes, 81
Summer Fruits Cupcakes, 24

BEETROOT
Chocolate Cigarillo Cupcakes, 73

BISCUITS, BOURBON
Chocolate Cookies and Cream Cupcakes, 93
Mint Cookie Cupcakes, 133

BISCUITS
Jam-filled Biscuit Cupcakes, 141

BLACKCURRANTS
Fruit and Cream Cupcakes, 213

BLUEBERRIES
Blueberry Cinnamon Cupcakes, 44
Blueberry Dream Cupcakes, 27
Blueberry Smile Cupcakes, 126
Sugared Blueberry Pie Cupcakes, 85
Summer Fruits Cupcakes, 24
Very Blueberry Cupcakes, 32

BUTTER
Baby Boots Cupcakes, 114
Banoffee Pie Cupcakes, 81
Beach Shoes Cupcakes, 117
Birthday Blues Cupcakes, 177
Black and White Cupcakes, 118
Blueberry Dream Cupcakes, 27
Blueberry Smile Cupcakes, 126
Camper-van Cupcakes, 121
Candles Cupcakes, 166
Candy Hearts Cupcakes, 194
Cappuccino Cupcakes, 94
Chocolate Ball Mint Cupcakes, 106
Chocolate Butterfly Cupcakes, 201
Chocolate Chip Cream Cupcakes, 74
Chocolate Cigarillo Cupcakes, 73
Chocolate Cola Bottle Cupcakes, 130
Chocolate Cookies and Cream Cupcakes, 93
Chocolate Decandence Cupcakes, 66
Chocolate Mint Sweetie Cupcakes, 105
Chocolate Raspberry Buttercream Cupcakes, 86
Chocolate Tear Cupcakes, 90
Choco-Latte Cupcakes, 202
Choco-Vanilla Cupcakes, 16
Coffee Truffle Cupcakes, 205
Coming Up Roses Cupcakes, 193
Crimson Raspberry Cupcakes, 51
Crown Cupcakes, 113
Dark Chocolate Delight Cupcakes, 82
Date and Rum Cupcakes, 35

Day Dream Cupcakes, 69
Double Chocolate Pillow Cupcakes, 36
Double Shot Cupcakes, 39
Dove Cupcakes, 142
Fondant Cherry Cupcakes, 149
Fruit and Cream Cupcakes, 213
Funky Toadstool Cupcakes, 122
Getting Piggy Cupcakes, 125
Gingerbread Man Cupcakes, 110
Glitter Magic Cupcakes, 174
Gluten-free Butterfly Cupcakes, 182
Greek Yoghurt Cupcakes, 48
Green Ribbon Cupcakes, 158
I Heart Chocolate, 181
Irresistible Dark Chocolate Cupcakes, 198
Jam-filled Biscuit Cupcakes, 141
Jelly Mint Cupcakes, 214
Jelly Sweet Temptation Cupcakes, 15
Kiwi Cupcakes, 101
Lavender Pillow Cupcakes, 97
Lemon and Poppy Seed Stars, 20
Lemon Drop Cupcakes, 77
Lime and Ginger Jelly Bean Cupcakes, 137
Macchiato Cupcakes, 102
Mint Cookie Cupcakes, 133
Mint Julep Cupcakes, 134
Mint Truffle Cupcakes, 218
Minty Heart Cupcakes, 150
Mochaccino Cupcakes, 98
Orange Jelly Ring Cupcakes, 129
Owl Cupcakes, 146
Pearls Cupcakes, 153
Pink Butterfly Cupcakes, 190
Pink Champagne Cupcakes, 154
Pink Crown Raspberry Cupcakes, 89
Polka Dot Cupcakes, 157
Popcorn Cupcakes, 58
Presents Cupcakes, 162
Pretzel Mania Cupcakes, 61
Raspberry Dream Cupcakes, 54
Raspberry Jelly Sweet Cupcakes, 206
Raspberry Mess Cupcakes, 62
Raspberry Yoghurt Cupcakes, 8
Red Sugar Cakes, 12
Red Velvet Heart Flower Cupcakes, 47
Sammy Snake Cupcakes, 185
Shooting Star Cupcakes, 161
Strawberry Jam-filled Cupcakes, 189
Strawberry Jam Frosted Cupcakes, 78
Strawberry Ripple Cupcakes, 186
Strawberry Surprise Cupcakes, 178
Sugared Blueberry Pie Cupcakes, 85
Sweet Dreams Cupcakes, 65
Sweet Treats Cupcakes, 197
Vanilla Chocolate Cupcakes, 19
Vanilla Cream Raspberry Cupcakes, 23
Vanilla Rose Cupcakes, 70
Vanilla Sprinkles Cakes, 173
Very Blueberry Cupcakes, 32
Violet Cream Cupcakes, 40
Violet Lemon Jelly Bean Cupcakes, 217
Walnut Cream Cupcakes, 28
White Choc Chip Dream Cupcakes, 11
White-Choc Coffee Cupcakes, 43
White Chocolate Raspberry Liquorice Cupcakes, 31

BUTTERMILK
Blueberry Dream Cupcakes, 27
Chocolate Cigarillo Cupcakes, 73
Glitter Magic Cupcakes, 174

CARROTS
Candy Hearts Cupcakes, 194

CHOCOLATE BALL SWEETS
Chocolate Ball Mint Cupcakes, 106
Chocolate Decandence Cupcakes, 66
Choco-Vanilla Cupcakes, 16
Macchiato Cupcakes, 102

CHOCOLATE BUTTONS
Chocolate Decandence Cupcakes, 66
Sweet Treats Cupcakes, 197
White-Choc Coffee Cupcakes, 43

CHOCOLATE CIGARILLOS
Cappuccino Cupcakes, 94
Chocolate Cigarillo Cupcakes, 73
Chocolate, Raspberry and Kiwi Cupcakes, 138

CHOCOLATE, DARK
Chocolate Decandence Cupcakes, 66
Dark Chocolate Delight Cupcakes, 82
I Heart Chocolate, 181
Mochaccino Cupcakes, 98
Raspberry Dream Cupcakes, 54
Vanilla Chocolate Cupcakes, 19

CHOCOLATE, MILK
Chocolate Chip Cream Cupcakes, 74
Choco-Latte Cupcakes, 202

CHOCOLATE, WHITE
Vanilla Chocolate Cupcakes, 19
White Choc Chip Dream Cupcakes, 11
White Chocolate Raspberry Liquorice Cupcakes, 31

CINNAMON
Birthday Blues Cupcakes, 177
Blueberry Cinnamon Cupcakes, 44
Candy Hearts Cupcakes, 194
Popcorn Cupcakes, 58
Red Velvet Heart Flower Cupcakes, 47

COCOA POWDER
Beach Shoes Cupcakes, 117
Butterfly Cupcakes, 170
Cappuccino Cupcakes, 94
Chocolate Ball Mint Cupcakes, 106
Chocolate Butterfly Cupcakes, 201
Chocolate Chip Cream Cupcakes, 74
Chocolate Cigarillo Cupcakes, 73
Chocolate Cola Bottle Cupcakes, 130
Chocolate Cookies and Cream Cupcakes, 93
Chocolate Decandence Cupcakes, 66
Chocolate Mint Sweetie Cupcakes, 105
Chocolate Raspberry Buttercream Cupcakes, 86
Chocolate Tear Cupcakes, 90
Choco-Latte Cupcakes, 202
Choco-Vanilla Cupcakes, 16
Coffee Truffle Cupcakes, 205
Dark Chocolate Delight Cupcakes, 82
Double Chocolate Pillow Cupcakes, 36
Fondant Cherry Cupcakes, 149
Funky Toadstool Cupcakes, 122
Green Ribbon Cupcakes, 158
I Heart Chocolate, 181
Irresistible Dark Chocolate Cupcakes, 198
Macchiato Cupcakes, 102
Mint Cookie Cupcakes, 133

Mint Truffle Cupcakes, 218
Mochaccino Cupcakes, 98
Pretzel Mania Cupcakes, 61
Vanilla Chocolate Cupcakes, 19
Vanilla Cream Raspberry Cupcakes, 23

COCONUT
Raspberry Mess Cupcakes, 62

COFFEE
Cappuccino Cupcakes, 94
Choco-Latte Cupcakes, 202
Coffee Truffle Cupcakes, 205
Double Shot Cupcakes, 39
Macchiato Cupcakes, 102
Mochaccino Cupcakes, 98
Raspberry Dream Cupcakes, 54
Walnut Cream Cupcakes, 28
White-Choc Coffee Cupcakes, 43

CREAM CHEESE
Blueberry Cinnamon Cupcakes, 44
Chocolate, Raspberry and Kiwi Cupcakes, 138
I Heart Chocolate, 181
Candy Hearts Cupcakes, 194
Red Velvet Heart Flower Cupcakes, 47
Sour Cream Cupcakes, 210
Strawberry Surprise Cupcakes, 178
Very Blueberry Cupcakes, 32

CREAM, DOUBLE (HEAVY)
Banoffee Pie Cupcakes, 81
Chocolate Ball Mint Cupcakes, 106
Chocolate Cola Bottle Cupcakes, 130

CREAM, SOUR
Sour Cream Cupcakes, 210

CREAM, WHIPPING
Raspberry Dream Cupcakes, 54

CRÈME FRAICHE
Summer Fruits Cupcakes, 24

CUSTARD POWDER
Strawberry Surprise Cupcakes, 178

DATES
Date and Rum Cupcakes, 35

DULCE DE LECHE
Popcorn Cupcakes, 58

EARL GREY TEA BAGS
Coming Up Roses Cupcakes, 193

EDIBLE GLITTER
Birthday Blues Cupcakes, 177
Candles Cupcakes, 166
Chocolate Tear Cupcakes, 90
Glitter Magic Cupcakes, 174
Greek Yoghurt Cupcakes, 48
Raspberry Yoghurt Cupcakes, 8
Red Velvet Heart Flower Cupcakes, 47

EGGS
Baby Boots Cupcakes, 114
Beach Shoes Cupcakes, 117
Birthday Blues Cupcakes, 177
Black and White Cupcakes, 118
Blueberry Cinnamon Cupcakes, 44

Blueberry Dream Cupcakes, 27
Blueberry Smile Cupcakes, 126
Butterfly Cupcakes, 170
Camper-van Cupcakes, 121
Candles Cupcakes, 166
Candy Hearts Cupcakes, 194
Cappuccino Cupcakes, 94
Chocolate Ball Mint Cupcakes, 106
Chocolate Butterfly Cupcakes, 201
Chocolate Chip Cream Cupcakes, 74
Chocolate Cigarillo Cupcakes, 73
Chocolate Cola Bottle Cupcakes, 130
Chocolate Cookies and Cream Cupcakes, 93
Chocolate Decandence Cupcakes, 66
Chocolate Mint Sweetie Cupcakes, 105
Chocolate, Raspberry and Kiwi Cupcakes, 138
Chocolate Raspberry Buttercream Cupcakes, 86
Chocolate Tear Cupcakes, 90
Choco-Latte Cupcakes, 202
Choco-Vanilla Cupcakes, 16
Coffee Truffle Cupcakes, 205
Coming Up Roses Cupcakes, 193
Crimson Raspberry Cupcakes, 51
Crown Cupcakes, 113
Dark Chocolate Delight Cupcakes, 82
Date and Rum Cupcakes, 35
Day Dream Cupcakes, 69
Double Chocolate Pillow Cupcakes, 36
Double Shot Cupcakes, 39
Dove Cupcakes, 142
Fondant Cherry Cupcakes, 149
Fruit and Cream Cupcakes, 213
Funky Toadstool Cupcakes, 122
Getting Piggy Cupcakes, 125
Gingerbread Man Cupcakes, 110
Glitter Magic Cupcakes, 174
Gluten-free Butterfly Cupcakes, 182
Greek Yoghurt Cupcakes, 48
Green Ribbon Cupcakes, 158
I Heart Chocolate, 181
Irresistible Dark Chocolate Cupcakes, 198
Jam-filled Biscuit Cupcakes, 141
Jelly Mint Cupcakes, 214
Jelly Sweet Temptation Cupcakes, 15
Kiwi Cupcakes, 101
Lavender Pillow Cupcakes, 97
Lemon and Poppy Seed Stars, 20
Lemon Drop Cupcakes, 77
Lime and Ginger Jelly Bean Cupcakes, 137
Macchiato Cupcakes, 102
Mint Cookie Cupcakes, 133
Mint Julep Cupcakes, 134
Mint Truffle Cupcakes, 218
Minty Heart Cupcakes, 150
Mochaccino Cupcakes, 98
Orange Jelly Ring Cupcakes, 129
Owl Cupcakes, 146
Pearls Cupcakes, 153
Pink Butterfly Cupcakes, 190
Pink Champagne Cupcakes, 154
Pink Crown Raspberry Cupcakes, 89
Pink Guitar Cupcakes, 145
Polka Dot Cupcakes, 157
Popcorn Cupcakes, 58
Presents Cupcakes, 162
Pretzel Mania Cupcakes, 61
Raspberry Dream Cupcakes, 54
Raspberry Jelly Sweet Cupcakes, 206
Raspberry Mess Cupcakes, 62
Raspberry Yoghurt Cupcakes, 8

Red Sugar Cakes, 12
Red Velvet Heart Flower Cupcakes, 47
Sammy Snake Cupcakes, 185
Shooting Star Cupcakes, 161
Sour Cream Cupcakes, 210
Strawberry Jam-filled Cupcakes, 189
Strawberry Jam Frosted Cupcakes, 78
Strawberry Ripple Cupcakes, 186
Strawberry Surprise Cupcakes, 178
Sugared Blueberry Pie Cupcakes, 85
Summer Fruits Cupcakes, 24
Sweet Dreams Cupcakes, 65
Sweet Treats Cupcakes, 197
Vanilla Chocolate Cupcakes, 19
Vanilla Cream Raspberry Cupcakes, 23
Vanilla Rose Cupcakes, 70
Vanilla Sprinkles Cakes, 173
Very Blueberry Cupcakes, 32
Violet Cream Cupcakes, 40
Violet Lemon Jelly Bean Cupcakes, 217
Walnut Cream Cupcakes, 28
White Choc Chip Dream Cupcakes, 11
White-Choc Coffee Cupcakes, 43
White Chocolate Raspberry Liquorice Cupcakes, 31

FLOUR, GLUTEN-FREE SELF-RAISING
Gluten-free Butterfly Cupcakes, 182

FLOUR, PLAIN (ALL PURPOSE)
Banoffee Pie Cupcakes, 81
Birthday Blues Cupcakes, 177
Blueberry Dream Cupcakes, 27
Chocolate Cigarillo Cupcakes, 73
Coming Up Roses Cupcakes, 193
Day Dream Cupcakes, 69
Funky Toadstool Cupcakes, 122
Glitter Magic Cupcakes, 174
I Heart Chocolate, 181
Pretzel Mania Cupcakes, 61
Strawberry Surprise Cupcakes, 178
Sweet Dreams Cupcakes, 65
Very Blueberry Cupcakes, 32
White Choc Chip Dream Cupcakes, 11
White Chocolate Raspberry Liquorice Cupcakes, 31

FLOUR, SELF-RAISING
Baby Boots Cupcakes, 114
Beach Shoes Cupcakes, 117
Black and White Cupcakes, 118
Blueberry Cinnamon Cupcakes, 44
Blueberry Smile Cupcakes, 126
Butterfly Cupcakes, 170
Camper-van Cupcakes, 121
Candles Cupcakes, 166
Candy Hearts Cupcakes, 194
Cappuccino Cupcakes, 94
Chocolate Ball Mint Cupcakes, 106
Chocolate Butterfly Cupcakes, 201
Chocolate Chip Cream Cupcakes, 74
Chocolate Cola Bottle Cupcakes, 130
Chocolate Cookies and Cream Cupcakes, 93
Chocolate Decandence Cupcakes, 66
Chocolate Mint Sweetie Cupcakes, 105
Chocolate, Raspberry and Kiwi Cupcakes, 138
Chocolate Raspberry Buttercream Cupcakes, 86
Chocolate Tear Cupcakes, 90
Choco-Latte Cupcakes, 202
Choco-Vanilla Cupcakes, 16

Coffee Truffle Cupcakes, 205
Crimson Raspberry Cupcakes, 51
Crown Cupcakes, 113
Dark Chocolate Delight Cupcakes, 82
Date and Rum Cupcakes, 35
Double Chocolate Pillow Cupcakes, 36
Double Shot Cupcakes, 39
Dove Cupcakes, 142
Fondant Cherry Cupcakes, 149
Fruit and Cream Cupcakes, 213
Getting Piggy Cupcakes, 125
Gingerbread Man Cupcakes, 110
Greek Yoghurt Cupcakes, 48
Green Ribbon Cupcakes, 158
Irresistible Dark Chocolate Cupcakes, 198
Jam-filled Biscuit Cupcakes, 141
Jelly Mint Cupcakes, 214
Jelly Sweet Temptation Cupcakes, 15
Kiwi Cupcakes, 101
Lavender Pillow Cupcakes, 97
Lemon and Poppy Seed Stars, 20
Lemon Drop Cupcakes, 77
Lime and Ginger Jelly Bean Cupcakes, 137
Macchiato Cupcakes, 102
Mint Cookie Cupcakes, 133
Mint Julep Cupcakes, 134
Mint Truffle Cupcakes, 218
Minty Heart Cupcakes, 150
Mochaccino Cupcakes, 98
Orange Jelly Ring Cupcakes, 129
Owl Cupcakes, 146
Pearls Cupcakes, 153
Pink Butterfly Cupcakes, 190
Pink Champagne Cupcakes, 154
Pink Crown Raspberry Cupcakes, 89
Pink Guitar Cupcakes, 145
Polka Dot Cupcakes, 157
Popcorn Cupcakes, 58
Presents Cupcakes, 162
Raspberry Dream Cupcakes, 54
Raspberry Jelly Sweet Cupcakes, 206
Raspberry Mess Cupcakes, 62
Raspberry Yoghurt Cupcakes, 8
Red Velvet Heart Flower Cupcakes, 47
Sammy Snake Cupcakes, 185
Shooting Star Cupcakes, 161
Sour Cream Cupcakes, 210
Strawberry Jam-filled Cupcakes, 189
Strawberry Jam Frosted Cupcakes, 78
Strawberry Ripple Cupcakes, 186
Sugared Blueberry Pie Cupcakes, 85
Summer Fruits Cupcakes, 24
Sweet Treats Cupcakes, 197
Vanilla Chocolate Cupcakes, 19
Vanilla Cream Raspberry Cupcakes, 23
Vanilla Rose Cupcakes, 70
Vanilla Sprinkles Cakes, 173
Violet Cream Cupcakes, 40
Violet Lemon Jelly Bean Cupcakes, 217
Walnut Cream Cupcakes, 28
White-Choc Coffee Cupcakes, 43

FLOUR, WHOLEMEAL
Candy Hearts Cupcakes, 194
Red Sugar Cakes, 12

FONDANT ICING
Baby Boots Cupcakes, 114
Beach Shoes Cupcakes, 117
Black and White Cupcakes, 118
Butterfly Cupcakes, 170

Camper-van Cupcakes, 121
Crown Cupcakes, 113
Dove Cupcakes, 142
Fondant Cherry Cupcakes, 149
Getting Piggy Cupcakes, 125
Gingerbread Man Cupcakes, 110
Green Ribbon Cupcakes, 158
Owl Cupcakes, 146
Pearls Cupcakes, 153
Pink Champagne Cupcakes, 154
Pink Guitar Cupcakes, 145
Polka Dot Cupcakes, 157
Presents Cupcakes, 162
Red Velvet Heart Flower Cupcakes, 47
Shooting Star Cupcakes, 161

FRAMBOISE LIQUEUR
Crimson Raspberry Cupcakes, 51
Pink Crown Raspberry Cupcakes, 89
White Chocolate Raspberry Liquorice
    Cupcakes, 31

GINGER
Candy Hearts Cupcakes, 194
Lime and Ginger Jelly Bean Cupcakes, 137
Vanilla Rose Cupcakes, 70

GINGER CORDIAL
Lime and Ginger Jelly Bean Cupcakes, 137

GOLDEN SYRUP
Popcorn Cupcakes, 58

GUINNESS STOUT
Pretzel Mania Cupcakes, 61

HUNDREDS AND THOUSANDS
Double Shot Cupcakes, 39
Irresistible Dark Chocolate Cupcakes, 198
Mint Truffle Cupcakes, 218

JAM (JELLY)
Jelly Sweet Temptation Cupcakes, 15
Pink Guitar Cupcakes, 145
Strawberry Jam-filled Cupcakes, 189
Strawberry Jam Frosted Cupcakes, 78

KIWI FRUIT
Chocolate, Raspberry and Kiwi Cupcakes, 138
Fruit and Cream Cupcakes, 213
Kiwi Cupcakes, 101

LAVENDER
Lavender Pillow Cupcakes, 97

LEMON
Blueberry Cinnamon Cupcakes, 44
Blueberry Smile Cupcakes, 126
Camper-van Cupcakes, 121
Crown Cupcakes, 113
Gingerbread Man Cupcakes, 110
Greek Yoghurt Cupcakes, 48
Lavender Pillow Cupcakes, 97
Lemon and Poppy Seed Stars, 20
Lemon Drop Cupcakes, 77
Owl Cupcakes, 146
Pearls Cupcakes, 153
Strawberry Surprise Cupcakes, 178
Violet Lemon Jelly Bean Cupcakes, 217

LEMON CURD
Lemon Drop Cupcakes, 77

LIME
Lime and Ginger Jelly Bean Cupcakes, 137

LOW-FAT SPREAD
Summer Fruits Cupcakes, 24

MARGARINE
Blueberry Cinnamon Cupcakes, 44
Blueberry Smile Cupcakes, 126
Cappuccino Cupcakes, 94
Chocolate Ball Mint Cupcakes, 106
Chocolate Butterfly Cupcakes, 201
Chocolate Cola Bottle Cupcakes, 130
Chocolate Cookies and Cream Cupcakes, 93
Chocolate Mint Sweetie Cupcakes, 105
Chocolate, Raspberry and Kiwi Cupcakes, 138
Chocolate Raspberry Buttercream Cupcakes,
    86
Chocolate Tear Cupcakes, 90
Choco-Latte Cupcakes, 202
Coffee Truffle Cupcakes, 205
Crimson Raspberry Cupcakes, 51
Date and Rum Cupcakes, 35
Double Chocolate Pillow Cupcakes, 36
Double Shot Cupcakes, 39
Fruit and Cream Cupcakes, 213
Getting Piggy Cupcakes, 125
Greek Yoghurt Cupcakes, 48
Jam-filled Biscuit Cupcakes, 141
Jelly Mint Cupcakes, 214
Kiwi Cupcakes, 101
Lavender Pillow Cupcakes, 97
Lime and Ginger Jelly Bean Cupcakes, 137
Macchiato Cupcakes, 102
Mint Cookie Cupcakes, 133
Mint Julep Cupcakes, 134
Mint Truffle Cupcakes, 218
Minty Heart Cupcakes, 150
Mochaccino Cupcakes, 98
Orange Jelly Ring Cupcakes, 129
Pink Crown Raspberry Cupcakes, 89
Pink Guitar Cupcakes, 145
Raspberry Jelly Sweet Cupcakes, 206
Raspberry Yoghurt Cupcakes, 8
Sammy Snake Cupcakes, 185
Sour Cream Cupcakes, 210
Sugared Blueberry Pie Cupcakes, 85
Sweet Treats Cupcakes, 197
Violet Cream Cupcakes, 40
Violet Lemon Jelly Bean Cupcakes, 217
White-Choc Coffee Cupcakes, 43

MARSHMALLOWS
Sweet Dreams Cupcakes, 65

MILK
Banoffee Pie Cupcakes, 81
Birthday Blues Cupcakes, 177
Cappuccino Cupcakes, 94
Chocolate Ball Mint Cupcakes, 106
Chocolate Butterfly Cupcakes, 201
Chocolate Chip Cream Cupcakes, 74
Chocolate Cola Bottle Cupcakes, 130
Chocolate Cookies and Cream Cupcakes, 93
Chocolate Mint Sweetie Cupcakes, 105
Chocolate Raspberry Buttercream Cupcakes,
    86
Chocolate Tear Cupcakes, 90

Choco-Vanilla Cupcakes, 16
Coffee Truffle Cupcakes, 205
Coming Up Roses Cupcakes, 193
Dark Chocolate Delight Cupcakes, 82
Double Chocolate Pillow Cupcakes, 36
Funky Toadstool Cupcakes, 122
Irresistible Dark Chocolate Cupcakes, 198
Lemon and Poppy Seed Stars, 20
Macchiato Cupcakes, 102
Mint Cookie Cupcakes, 133
Mochaccino Cupcakes, 98
Pink Butterfly Cupcakes, 190
Popcorn Cupcakes, 58
Pretzel Mania Cupcakes, 61
Raspberry Mess Cupcakes, 62
Red Sugar Cakes, 12
Sammy Snake Cupcakes, 185
Strawberry Jam-filled Cupcakes, 189
Sweet Dreams Cupcakes, 65
Vanilla Cream Raspberry Cupcakes, 23
Vanilla Sprinkles Cakes, 173
Very Blueberry Cupcakes, 32
Walnut Cream Cupcakes, 28
White Choc Chip Dream Cupcakes, 11
White Chocolate Raspberry Liquorice
   Cupcakes, 31

MINTS
Chocolate Mint Sweetie Cupcakes, 105

ORANGE
Banoffee Pie Cupcakes, 81
Candy Hearts Cupcakes, 194

ORANGE FLOWER WATER
Orange Jelly Ring Cupcakes, 129

PEPPERMINT EXTRACT
Chocolate Ball Mint Cupcakes, 106
Chocolate Mint Sweetie Cupcakes, 105
Jelly Mint Cupcakes, 214
Mint Cookie Cupcakes, 133
Mint Julep Cupcakes, 134
Mint Truffle Cupcakes, 218
Minty Heart Cupcakes, 150

PHYSALIS
Fruit and Cream Cupcakes, 213

POPCORN
Popcorn Cupcakes, 58

POPPY SEEDS
Lemon and Poppy Seed Stars, 20

PRETZELS
Pretzel Mania Cupcakes, 61

RASPBERRIES
Chocolate, Raspberry and Kiwi Cupcakes, 138
Chocolate Raspberry Buttercream Cupcakes,
   86
Crimson Raspberry Cupcakes, 51
Fruit and Cream Cupcakes, 213
Pink Crown Raspberry Cupcakes, 89
Raspberry Dream Cupcakes, 54
Raspberry Mess Cupcakes, 62
Raspberry Yoghurt Cupcakes, 8
Summer Fruits Cupcakes, 24
Vanilla Cream Raspberry Cupcakes, 23

RASPBERRY LIQUORICE
White Chocolate Raspberry Liquorice
   Cupcakes, 31

RHUBARB
Vanilla Rose Cupcakes, 70

RUM
Date and Rum Cupcakes, 35

STRAWBERRIES
Pink Butterfly Cupcakes, 190
Strawberry Ripple Cupcakes, 186
Strawberry Surprise Cupcakes, 178

STRAWBERRIES, FREEZE-DRIED
Strawberry Jam Frosted Cupcakes, 78

STRAWBERRY ESSENCE
Pink Butterfly Cupcakes, 190

SUGAR, BROWN
Beach Shoes Cupcakes, 117
Birthday Blues Cupcakes, 177
Popcorn Cupcakes, 58
White Choc Chip Dream Cupcakes, 11

SUGAR, CASTER (SUPERFINE)
Baby Boots Cupcakes, 114
Banoffee Pie Cupcakes, 81
Beach Shoes Cupcakes, 117
Birthday Blues Cupcakes, 177
Black and White Cupcakes, 118
Blueberry Cinnamon Cupcakes, 44
Blueberry Dream Cupcakes, 27
Blueberry Smile Cupcakes, 126
Butterfly Cupcakes, 170
Camper-van Cupcakes, 121
Candles Cupcakes, 166
Cappuccino Cupcakes, 94
Chocolate Ball Mint Cupcakes, 106
Chocolate Butterfly Cupcakes, 201
Chocolate Cola Bottle Cupcakes, 130
Chocolate Cookies and Cream Cupcakes, 93
Chocolate Decandence Cupcakes, 66
Chocolate Mint Sweetie Cupcakes, 105
Chocolate, Raspberry and Kiwi Cupcakes, 138
Chocolate Raspberry Buttercream Cupcakes,
   86
Chocolate Tear Cupcakes, 90
Choco-Latte Cupcakes, 202
Choco-Vanilla Cupcakes, 16
Coffee Truffle Cupcakes, 205
Coming Up Roses Cupcakes, 193
Crimson Raspberry Cupcakes, 51
Crown Cupcakes, 113
Dark Chocolate Delight Cupcakes, 82
Date and Rum Cupcakes, 35
Double Chocolate Pillow Cupcakes, 36
Double Shot Cupcakes, 39
Dove Cupcakes, 142
Fondant Cherry Cupcakes, 149
Fruit and Cream Cupcakes, 213
Funky Toadstool Cupcakes, 122
Getting Piggy Cupcakes, 125
Gingerbread Man Cupcakes, 110
Glitter Magic Cupcakes, 174
Gluten Free Butterfly Cupcakes, 182
Greek Yoghurt Cupcakes, 48
Green Ribbon Cupcakes, 158
I Heart Chocolate, 181

Irresistible Dark Chocolate Cupcakes, 198
Jam-filled Biscuit Cupcakes, 141
Jelly Mint Cupcakes, 214
Jelly Sweet Temptation Cupcakes, 15
Kiwi Cupcakes, 101
Lavender Pillow Cupcakes, 97
Lemon and Poppy Seed Stars, 20
Lemon Drop Cupcakes, 77
Lime and Ginger Jelly Bean Cupcakes, 137
Macchiato Cupcakes, 102
Mint Cookie Cupcakes, 133
Mint Julep Cupcakes, 134
Mint Truffle Cupcakes, 218
Minty Heart Cupcakes, 150
Mochaccino Cupcakes, 98
Orange Jelly Ring Cupcakes, 129
Owl Cupcakes, 146
Pearls Cupcakes, 153
Pink Butterfly Cupcakes, 190
Pink Champagne Cupcakes, 154
Pink Crown Raspberry Cupcakes, 89
Pink Guitar Cupcakes, 145
Polka Dot Cupcakes, 157
Presents Cupcakes, 162
Raspberry Jelly Sweet Cupcakes, 206
Raspberry Mess Cupcakes, 62
Raspberry Yoghurt Cupcakes, 8
Red Velvet Heart Flower Cupcakes, 47
Sammy Snake Cupcakes, 185
Shooting Star Cupcakes, 161
Sour Cream Cupcakes, 210
Strawberry Jam-filled Cupcakes, 189
Strawberry Jam Frosted Cupcakes, 78
Strawberry Ripple Cupcakes, 186
Strawberry Surprise Cupcakes, 178
Sugared Blueberry Pie Cupcakes, 85
Sweet Dreams Cupcakes, 65
Sweet Treats Cupcakes, 197
Vanilla Chocolate Cupcakes, 19
Vanilla Cream Raspberry Cupcakes, 23
Vanilla Sprinkles Cakes, 173
Violet Cream Cupcakes, 40
Violet Lemon Jelly Bean Cupcakes, 217
White-Choc Coffee Cupcakes, 43
White Chocolate Raspberry Liquorice
   Cupcakes, 31

SUGAR CRYSTALS
Violet Cream Cupcakes, 40

SUGAR, GRANULATED
Chocolate Cigarillo Cupcakes, 73
Day Dream Cupcakes, 69
Lemon Drop Cupcakes, 77
Pretzel Mania Cupcakes, 61
Red Sugar Cakes, 12
Very Blueberry Cupcakes, 32
White Choc Chip Dream Cupcakes, 11

SUGAR, HALF SPOON GRANULATED
Summer Fruits Cupcakes, 24

SUGAR, ICING (CONFECTIONERS')
Baby Boots Cupcakes, 114
Birthday Blues Cupcakes, 177
Black and White Cupcakes, 118
Blueberry Cinnamon Cupcakes, 44
Blueberry Dream Cupcakes, 27
Blueberry Smile Cupcakes, 126
Butterfly Cupcakes, 170
Candles Cupcakes, 166

Cappuccino Cupcakes, 94
Chocolate Ball Mint Cupcakes, 106
Chocolate Butterfly Cupcakes, 201
Chocolate Chip Cream Cupcakes, 74
Chocolate Cigarillo Cupcakes, 73
Chocolate Cola Bottle Cupcakes, 130
Chocolate Cookies and Cream Cupcakes, 93
Chocolate Decandence Cupcakes, 66
Chocolate Mint Sweetie Cupcakes, 105
Chocolate, Raspberry and Kiwi Cupcakes, 138
Chocolate Raspberry Buttercream Cupcakes, 86
Chocolate Tear Cupcakes, 90
Choco-Vanilla Cupcakes, 16
Coffee Truffle Cupcakes, 205
Coming Up Roses Cupcakes, 193
Crimson Raspberry Cupcakes, 51
Crown Cupcakes, 113
Dark Chocolate Delight Cupcakes, 82
Date and Rum Cupcakes, 35
Day Dream Cupcakes, 69
Double Chocolate Pillow Cupcakes, 36
Double Shot Cupcakes, 39
Dove Cupcakes, 142
Fondant Cherry Cupcakes, 149
Fruit and Cream Cupcakes, 213
Funky Toadstool Cupcakes, 122
Getting Piggy Cupcakes, 125
Gingerbread Man Cupcakes, 110
Glitter Magic Cupcakes, 174
Gluten-free Butterfly Cupcakes, 182
Greek Yoghurt Cupcakes, 48
Green Ribbon Cupcakes, 158
I Heart Chocolate, 181
Irresistible Dark Chocolate Cupcakes, 198
Jam-filled Biscuit Cupcakes, 141
Jelly Mint Cupcakes, 214
Jelly Sweet Temptation Cupcakes, 15
Kiwi Cupcakes, 101
Lavender Pillow Cupcakes, 97
Lemon and Poppy Seed Stars, 20
Lemon Drop Cupcakes, 77
Lime and Ginger Jelly Bean Cupcakes, 137
Candy Hearts Cupcakes, 194
Macchiato Cupcakes, 102
Mint Cookie Cupcakes, 133
Mint Julep Cupcakes, 134
Mint Truffle Cupcakes, 218
Minty Heart Cupcakes, 150
Mochaccino Cupcakes, 98
Orange Jelly Ring Cupcakes, 129
Pink Butterfly Cupcakes, 190
Pink Champagne Cupcakes, 154
Pink Crown Raspberry Cupcakes, 89
Popcorn Cupcakes, 58
Polka Dot Cupcakes, 157
Presents Cupcakes, 162
Pretzel Mania Cupcakes, 61
Raspberry Jelly Sweet Cupcakes, 206
Raspberry Mess Cupcakes, 62
Raspberry Yoghurt Cupcakes, 8
Red Sugar Cakes, 12
Red Velvet Heart Flower Cupcakes, 47
Sammy Snake Cupcakes, 185
Shooting Star Cupcakes, 161
Sour Cream Cupcakes, 210
Strawberry Jam-filled Cupcakes, 189
Strawberry Jam Frosted Cupcakes, 78
Strawberry Ripple Cupcakes, 186
Strawberry Surprise Cupcakes, 178
Sugared Blueberry Pie Cupcakes, 85

Sweet Dreams Cupcakes, 65
Sweet Treats Cupcakes, 197
Vanilla Chocolate Cupcakes, 19
Vanilla Cream Raspberry Cupcakes, 23
Vanilla Rose Cupcakes, 70
Vanilla Sprinkles Cakes, 173
Very Blueberry Cupcakes, 32
Violet Cream Cupcakes, 40
Violet Lemon Jelly Bean Cupcakes, 217
Walnut Cream Cupcakes, 28
White Choc Chip Dream Cupcakes, 11
White-Choc Coffee Cupcakes, 43
White Chocolate Raspberry Liquorice Cupcakes, 31

SUGAR, MUSCOVADO
Candy Hearts Cupcakes, 194
Chocolate Chip Cream Cupcakes, 74
Raspberry Dream Cupcakes, 54
Red Sugar Cakes, 12
Vanilla Rose Cupcakes, 70
Walnut Cream Cupcakes, 28

SUGAR SPRINKLES
Vanilla Sprinkles Cakes, 173

SUGARPASTE FLOWERS
Coming Up Roses Cupcakes, 193
Greek Yoghurt Cupcakes, 48
Strawberry Ripple Cupcakes, 186

SWEETS
Candy Hearts Cupcakes, 194
Chocolate Cola Bottle Cupcakes, 130
Day Dream Cupcakes, 69
Getting Piggy Cupcakes, 125
Jam-filled Biscuit Cupcakes, 141
Jelly Mint Cupcakes, 214
Jelly Sweet Temptation Cupcakes, 15
Lime and Ginger Jelly Bean Cupcakes, 137
Mint Julep Cupcakes, 134
Mint Truffle Cupcakes, 218
Minty Heart Cupcakes, 150
Orange Jelly Ring Cupcakes, 129
Pink Guitar Cupcakes, 145
Raspberry Jelly Sweet Cupcakes, 206
Sweet Treats Cupcakes, 197
Violet Lemon Jelly Bean Cupcakes, 217

VANILLA
Baby Boots Cupcakes, 114
Banoffee Pie Cupcakes, 81
Birthday Blues Cupcakes, 177
Black and White Cupcakes, 118
Blueberry Cinnamon Cupcakes, 44
Blueberry Dream Cupcakes, 27
Blueberry Smile Cupcakes, 126
Butterfly Cupcakes, 170
Candles Cupcakes, 166
Candy Hearts Cupcakes, 194
Chocolate Ball Mint Cupcakes, 106
Chocolate Butterfly Cupcakes, 201
Chocolate Chip Cream Cupcakes, 74
Chocolate Cigarillo Cupcakes, 73
Chocolate Cola Bottle Cupcakes, 130
Chocolate, Raspberry and Kiwi Cupcakes, 138
Choco-Latte Cupcakes, 202
Choco-Vanilla Cupcakes, 16
Coming Up Roses Cupcakes, 193
Crimson Raspberry Cupcakes, 51
Dark Chocolate Delight Cupcakes, 82

Date and Rum Cupcakes, 35
Day Dream Cupcakes, 69
Double Shot Cupcakes, 39
Dove Cupcakes, 142
Fondant Cherry Cupcakes, 149
Fruit and Cream Cupcakes, 213
Getting Piggy Cupcakes, 125
Glitter Magic Cupcakes, 174
Gluten-free Butterfly Cupcakes, 182
Greek Yoghurt Cupcakes, 48
Green Ribbon Cupcakes, 158
I Heart Chocolate, 181
Jam-filled Biscuit Cupcakes, 141
Jelly Mint Cupcakes, 214
Jelly Sweet Temptation Cupcakes, 15
Kiwi Cupcakes, 101
Lavender Pillow Cupcakes, 97
Lemon Drop Cupcakes, 77
Lime and Ginger Jelly Bean Cupcakes, 137
Mint Julep Cupcakes, 134
Mint Truffle Cupcakes, 218
Minty Heart Cupcakes, 150
Pink Butterfly Cupcakes, 190
Pink Champagne Cupcakes, 154
Pink Crown Raspberry Cupcakes, 89
Pink Guitar Cupcakes, 145
Polka Dot Cupcakes, 157
Popcorn Cupcakes, 58
Presents Cupcakes, 162
Pretzel Mania Cupcakes, 61
Raspberry Dream Cupcakes, 54
Raspberry Jelly Sweet Cupcakes, 206
Raspberry Mess Cupcakes, 62
Raspberry Yoghurt Cupcakes, 8
Red Sugar Cakes, 12
Red Velvet Heart Flower Cupcakes, 47
Sammy Snake Cupcakes, 185
Shooting Star Cupcakes, 161
Sour Cream Cupcakes, 210
Strawberry Jam-filled Cupcakes, 189
Strawberry Jam Frosted Cupcakes, 78
Strawberry Ripple Cupcakes, 186
Strawberry Surprise Cupcakes, 178
Sugared Blueberry Pie Cupcakes, 85
Sweet Dreams Cupcakes, 65
Vanilla Chocolate Cupcakes, 19
Vanilla Cream Raspberry Cupcakes, 23
Vanilla Rose Cupcakes, 70
Vanilla Sprinkles Cakes, 173
Very Blueberry Cupcakes, 32
Violet Cream Cupcakes, 40
Walnut Cream Cupcakes, 28
White Choc Chip Dream Cupcakes, 11
White-Choc Coffee Cupcakes, 43
White Chocolate Raspberry Liquorice Cupcakes, 31

VIOLET EXTRACT
Violet Lemon Jelly Bean Cupcakes, 217

WALNUTS
Walnut Cream Cupcakes, 28

YOGHURT
Greek Yoghurt Cupcakes, 48
Lemon and Poppy Seed Stars, 20
Raspberry Yoghurt Cupcakes, 8